JE T'AIME, ME NEITHER

April Lily Heise

D1600478

JE T'AIME, ME NEITHER

ISBN-13 : 978-0992005306
ISBN-10 : 0992005302

Cover Design and interior art by Aurélie Dhuit
www.aureliedhuit.com

Author photo by Pascale V. Marquis
http://pascalevmarquis.wix.com/site-3

All names (besides mine) and most cafés or bars in this book have been modified in order to protect their identity (and possibly reputation).

Publisher:
TGRS Communications
21 Allen Avenue,
Toronto, Ontario
Canada M4M 1T5

Email : jetaimemeneither@gmail.com
www.jetaimemeneither.com

This book is dedicated to all the girls for their endless support, and to all the boys, who—for better or worse—made this book happen . . .

CONTENTS

JE NE T'AIME PLUS

STEPHANE [04/10/2005 2:42 PM]
Are we still on for tonight?
We need to talk.

"Je ne t'aime plus."

What do you mean . . . you don't love *me anymore?* I sat there, dumbfounded, staring at my boyfriend—or rather, my **ex**-boyfriend—his words slowly sinking in. Once they had, the emotional floodgate opened, unleashing hot tears streaming down my cheeks.

What did he just say? He had never said that he *did* love me, so how could he *not* love me anymore? While I was trying to grapple with this unpleasant detail, another one hit me. *Hey! I was being broken up with!* This made me cry even harder.

Here I was, in my tiny Parisian apartment, overlooking the eternal City of *Amour*, which had just transformed into the City of *Désamour*, as I was now unloved, dumped, ditched, or, in French: *larguée*.

This wasn't how things were supposed to happen.

PARIS JE T'AIME . . .?

ROBERTO [04/12/05 12:05 AM]
A beautiful woman in Paris will
always attract the attention of men!
Big kiss, Roberto

"*MEN!*"

"I'm okay, Naughty. It's really for the best." I sighed, looking into my empty wine glass.

"You're right, you don't want to date a Frenchie anyway," declared Special Kay, topping me up. "They only tear out girls' hearts and rip them to pieces!" And with that severe statement, she emptied the rest of the bottle into her glass.

"Hey! You forgot me!" piped up Pussycat, holding out her equally dry glass, and with that we uncorked another bottle of *Saint Amour*. At least our favorite beverage would always be there for us, but would this be the only place we'd find a little *amour*?

My sad eyes drifted from my faithful friends towards the window. My *chambre de bonne* apartment (former maid's quarters) situated under the rooftops of Montmartre might have been tiny, but the impressive view went on forever. Out there was a majestic, twinkling city—full of passionate promise. I couldn't help but agree that Paris really was the romantic capital of the world. It wasn't just the beautiful buildings and picturesque passageways. There was something more, a special ambience that the city exuded. Love could practically be found around every corner, and romantic impulses could strike at any moment: a chance encounter in a park with a sexy stranger . . . a flirtatious *bonjour* . . . an offer to grab a drink. These were the sort of events my dear friend Roberto noted in his text message, sent from the opposite side of the *métro* platform while surveying how the passenger next to me was checking me out, edging closer and closer to me, preparing to make a move.

Was this passion merely the way of the city, or was it something rooted in French culture? I thought it had to be a bit of both, or at least a case of cause and effect. Did the French live for love? Were they more passionate—in all senses of the word—than other nationalities? French *amour*, in its most intense forms, has been expressed throughout the ages in fables, literature, art, film and song: the 11th-Century loyal lovers Abélard and Héloïse; the powerful mistresses of the kings; and, of course, the tortured Victorian-era fictional heroine Madame Bovary. For me, the anti-hero of the sexual revolution, Serge Gainsbourg, and his erotic, contradictory song—*Je t'aime, moi non plus* (I Love You, Me Neither)—summed up the situation accurately. The power of love can compel a French person to quickly throw out a "*je t'aime!*" after only a few dates, but the reverse passion can just as easily incite them to declare a "*je ne t'aime plus*" . . .

Such was my current predicament, but why? I seemed to have had this sort of very innate "*je t'aime, je ne t'aime plus*" and other strong French tendencies in me since the minute I was born . . .

I was convinced that the stork must have downed one glass of *rosé* too many on that hot August night when he delivered me. Instead of gently setting me down in an elegant Parisian apartment, with carefully polished parquet floors, molded ceilings and large "French" windows overlooking the Seine (and why not throw in the Eiffel Tower, too), I got plunked down on an old farm, in the middle of nowhere: rural Canada.

I couldn't have been further from my "true" home. Bohemian cafés and tree-lined boulevards had been swapped with rolling fields and endless forests; baguettes and Camembert were eclipsed by fresh corn on the cob and cheddar cheese. Nevertheless, my "French-ness" began manifesting itself at a young age.

At five, I held dainty tea parties for my French *poupées* (wine replaced tea in the adult versions with my Parisian *amies*). At nine, I ended up enrolled in the very first French immersion program in my tiny country town (I ask myself often if it was started just for me). At 12, I dressed up as a "fancy lady from Paris" for Halloween (a little more of the *real* me coming out). At 16, a psychic prophetically foretold me living and finding love in a faraway land (concrete proof!). I thus immediately set out to find a way to Europe and managed to send myself away on a student exchange. Well, I ended up in Italy instead of France, but I was getting close, and was teased by a one-week class trip to Paris with my Italian school: I was in a state of *je t'aime* bliss! At university, I finally succeeded in living in Paris, once again on a semester abroad (though I can't say we seriously studied anything besides French oenology and the best ways to flirt with the cute Argentinean boys in our residence). I was truly in seventh heaven, in perfect *paradis*. I knew I'd found my rightful home and would live one day *je t'aime*-ingly ever after.

After university, I found that the fastest way back to Paris (without having to marry myself off) was to sustain myself through various means. I did everything from teaching English for a school I found out was owned by Scientologists (a revelation learned only after locking myself into a long-term contract), to working another teaching gig at a faraway suburban university run by a creepy womanizer. Then there was translating painfully boring medical articles interspersed with a slightly more glamorous stint as a horribly under-paid art gallery slave. What I did for a living didn't really matter: I was in *my* city.

But here I was receiving a *je ne t'aime pas*. Did my city really **not** love me anymore? Its sparking optimism told another story. My gaze wandered back into the room and to *les filles*. I struggled out a smile. At least the girls—and the *Saint Amour*—would help me forget my current woes.

"Come on, cheer up!" pepped Pussycat.

"Lily, you know what you need? A spicy summer fling. Spring is in full swing. The ground is perfectly fertile, ready for sowing a few seeds of *amouuur*, ripe for the picking in summer," said Naughty—quite, well, naughtily. "That will make you forget about Stéphane in no time."

Stéphane—the source of my present heartache. In all honesty, the flame between me and my unaffectionate ex-boyfriend (how oddly un-French) had been dwindling for some time. My natural French-ness should have allowed me to confidently declare, "*je ne t'aime plus.*" Unfortunately, that particular capacity was over-ruled by my Canadian indecisiveness and passivity, which made me completely incapable of breaking up with anyone. I usually resorted to the cowardly tactic of not returning phone calls, or texting ridiculous excuses as to why I was suddenly never available (washing my hair, babysitting a friend's pet iguana, off in the Arctic protecting baby seals . . . to name a few). I had even once shamefully broken up with someone by posted letter (which horrifically arrived on Valentine's Day, even though I'd planned for it to arrive several days *before*. Curse you, late postal service!). Yet, after dating for nearly two years, Stéphane and I had passed the point where any of those awful maneuvers would be even mildly acceptable. This break up had to be done in person and, in the end, he'd beat me to the "*je ne t'aime plus.*" I actually wasn't really heartbroken; I had a serious case of "bruised ego blues."

Gazing down into my now half-empty glass of *Saint Amour*, it was almost like it was smiling up at me, agreeing with Naughty's idea with chipper exclamations: *Yes! A summer fling would be perfect! Exciting! Adventurous!* That is exactly how a little fling should be and that is precisely what the French call it: *une aventure*. The love vibes of the city could surely throw an attractive, fun, interesting *homme* my way. The sensual wheels of my mind began to spin wildly.

"Well, girls, what's life without a little *aventure*?" I finally replied with sassy conviction, ready to take on the challenge. In fact, I already had the perfect candidate in mind . . .

A MAYAN GOD UNDER THE PARISIAN SUMMER SUN

— I'll dance if you sing —

Private dances, concerts and serenading . . . this was what a summer fling was supposed to be all about. May my quest begin!

Since living in Paris, I'd tried my best to have French friends, and somewhat succeeded in befriending a few *Parisiennes* (and befriending—and romancing—even more *Parisiens*). Nevertheless, my world tended to revolve around the expatriate crowd. Case in point? The girls: Naughty, a seductive dance student from Toronto who'd earned her nickname from enticing boys on the dance-floor merely to practice her new moves; Pussycat, a secretly seductive photographer from Montréal; and Special Kay, a former cheerleader turned health-nut from California.

Over the last few years, I'd been organizing social activities for "the Canadian Club"—a group of hodge-podge expats— rather than just Canadians. While we did all kinds of non-Canadian things, one of our main activities was a monthly meet-up at a Canadian pub called *The Reindeer*. Located in the fashionable Saint Germain area, it was a place of stark contrast to the chic neighboring Parisian cafés. As soon as you walked through its door, you were instantly transported into an overwhelming Canadian cliché, with sports paraphernalia plastering the walls and pseudo-Canadian specialties on the menu . . . but a little taste of our native land did us good now and then.

I have to admit that I favored meeting at this kitschy bar mainly because I had a secret crush (well, my adoration might not have been completely secretive) on a particularly attractive bartender who worked there. He didn't look very "Canadian"; he was far from the broad-shouldered hockey-player types found working in most *real* Canadian bars. This was not to his detriment: his different looks gave him extra bonus points in my book. He had a nicely muscular build, olive skin, dark silky hair tucked behind his ears, and a killer smile . . . the perfect image of a seductive garden/pool boy. He fit the "fun summer fling" bill to a T.

After a bit of investigating, I found out that he was indeed not Canadian, but Mexican. Odd that he was working in a Canadian pub and not a Mexican one; he was totally adorable, I didn't care one *peso* where he came from. Being Mexican actually upped his value for me, and it gave him an exotic edge! In addition to his dashing good looks, he was always extremely sweet to me and often slipped me free drinks— a man after my own heart! Was he just being kind or did we share a mutual attraction? I was determined to find out.

I took extra care getting myself ready for my first "being single" pub night. I had to dress to impress, or rather, to seduce. No casual Canadian-wear for me. That said, it was only a Wednesday night (a.k.a. more of a casual night) so I couldn't look like I was trying too hard. I thus opted for a cute floral skirt and a slightly low-cut black top. This might be the right combo to capture some south-of-the-border prey. It was time to spice up my life with a little *caliente* Mexican seasoning!

I waltzed into the pub in the most nonchalant way I could, trying not to look directly at the bar where my sexy bartender would be. My bait worked, for I instantly caught his eye.

"Hey there, Lily *la Tigresse!*" he shouted enthusiastically. I turned my head in his direction, feigning surprise at seeing him, then strutted over to the bar to say hello.

"Wow! Don't you look pretty tonight!" he complimented, leaning over the bar to give me a kiss on each cheek, surely inflaming them. *You are also looking absolutely divine, Mr. Sexy Bartender,* I thought.

After making it through some petty small talk without fainting, I swooned over to the girls . . . "Isn't he *sooo* cute?"

"Lily, stay away from bar boys. You should know better. They're nothing but trouble," warned Naughty. "And besides, you don't even know his name."

"Since when has that ever stopped *you?*" I scoffed back. "Remember, I'm just looking for a little pick-me-up *fling.*"

Nonetheless, this time she was right; I didn't have the slightest clue as to Mr. Sexy Bartender's name and I couldn't very well just go around calling him "Mr. Sexy Bartender." But this was not a huge problem; his name could easily be obtained. It just so happened that we were hanging out near the bar, so I discretely listened for any name-calling from the other side.

"Hey, Sam, two pints over here." *Sam?* Well, there you go, his name was Sam. He didn't really look like a Sam and it wasn't a very Spanish-sounding name, but did it really matter?

Sexy Sam, Seductive Sam, Succulent Sam . . . it had a nice ring to it.

I was totally smitten. Sam was more than perfect for my summer fling. To achieve my goal, I started hanging out at *The Reindeer* at least once a week, sometimes twice. I even succeeded in finding out which nights he worked, and dragged the girls there as often as I could, and it seemed that on each new visit, the flirt meter fluttered higher and higher. Despite this, words never turned into actions. What did I have to do to win him over? Something would have to give, and soon.

"Lily, he could just be flirting for more tips. He's a bartender in France after all; he needs to work extra hard for them over here," said Naughty, who was still totally against my Mexican heartthrob. "He may even have a girlfriend, which we all know certainly doesn't stop guys in Paris from flirting with other girls."

"Stop spoiling my fun! Haven't you seen the way he looks at me? And he's 10,000 times nicer to me than he is to anyone else," I retorted, attempting to plead my case.

"Is that so? Well perhaps you're blinded by love, but he keeps going over to talk to that girl sitting at the end of the bar."

I wasn't blind at all. In fact, I *had* noticed that Sam had been chatting a lot to this other girl sitting all by herself at the end of the bar . . . very, very suspicious. I hadn't seen her around before . . . who could she be? I had to stay calm, as cool as a Cosmo. I could not let myself be overcome by jealousy. Ordering another cocktail would help my nerves . . . and tear Sam away from the possible threat. I flagged him down in the least desperate way possible.

While he was making my drink, I fished around for some

answers. "So, what have you been up to these days?" I coyly inquired, leaning seductively against the bar.

"Actually, I've been showing my cousin around, and practicing for the concert."

I gave Naughty an "I told you so" smirk. Obviously the girl at the end of the bar was his cousin and not his *girlfriend*. And did I catch the second part right? *A concert?*

"*Ohhhhh*, when's your concert?"

"We're playing for the 80's theme party in two weeks," he announced, proudly pointing to the nearby poster. "Are you coming?"

"Of course we are, aren't we?" I enthusiastically confirmed, alternately nodding my head at both Sam and Naughty.

"I guess we are . . . now," Naughty smugly conceded.

Wow! Sam was a musician, how exciting, how sexy! I imaged myself being serenaded with love songs in Spanish while lazily lounging in a beautiful Parisian park—perfect summer-fling-ness. And through more flirtatious chatting, I also discovered that he was not just a bartender, but was actually only working there to put himself through business school. Creative, smart, hardworking, charming, I was totally sold! . . . And counting down the days until the 80's night.

Paris in the springtime is absolutely the best time of the year to be in love. The city suddenly awakens from hibernation. After the chilly gray winter months, everyone's sexual appetites stir. Short skirts pop out of closets about as quickly as the cherry trees bloom, much to the approval of eager male admirers, allowing Paris to regain its title as the city of *amour* after a long winter's rest. With all that love in the air, it was easy for me to be swept up in the excitement.

One especially lovely sunny afternoon, the weather was just too nice for me to take the *métro* to my next appointment, so I decided to walk, soaking up the glorious rays along the way. I haphazardly chose my path, following the sunniest streets, and eventually ended up around Les Halles, a busy pedestrian area in central Paris, home to a dilapidated shopping mall and narrow streets lined with cheap street-wear clothes shops. All of this tackiness and hustle and bustle were completely eclipsed by the gorgeous weather.

As I strolled through the crowded streets, I was pulled out of my sunny dreams by the sight of an amazing dark-haired cutie, armed with a guitar, walking straight towards me. Stunned, it took me a minute to decide whether I'd come across either the reincarnation of the Mayan god of music or . . . *Sam?* Could it really be him? Our paths crossing in such a hectic area—was this destiny calling? The deity in question also did a double-take when he saw me. Realizing he had seen correctly (that he was indeed approaching a charming northern princess), a huge, handsome smile spread across his face. He seemed absolutely thrilled to see me, too. He was with some friends, but took a second to say "hi" and give me *la bise*, the French cheek kiss, before we rushed off in our respective directions.

That completely made my day! I was probably the happiest person on earth . . . or at least in Paris! Being a staunch believer in fate, I took this chance encounter as a definite sign that something was bound to and *meant* to happen between us.

I dragged Naughty, Pussycat and Special Kay to the 80's night, but the bar was so packed that I didn't have many chances to talk to Sam. Even so, Sam's performance was spectacular and the more I saw him, the more I was 100%

positive that he was destined to be my fling (or maybe even more!). As convinced as I was, I did realize that there was a tiny glitch in my plans—why hadn't he made a move? He really seemed to like me (as more than a friend) and I'd given him plenty of opportunities to ask me out. Maybe he was shy? Cautious about putting moves on clients? Naughty suggested that he might even be gay, but then again, she thought half the guys in Paris were gay (I had to admit, they often could be a bit on the feminine side). Or could it be that he had . . . a *girlfriend?*

During the next Canadian Club get-together at *The Reindeer,* I made the mistake of mentioning my concern to Naughty, who promptly took it upon herself to find out the truth. "When he's not around, I'll just ask one of the waitresses if he's already taken," she schemed.

"Not if I'm here to stop you!" I was completely against her plot, but my pleas fell on deaf ears. I didn't want the bar staff to think I was the reason behind her inquiring; it seemed like junior high school antics, and I didn't want to be the pathetic drooling admirer of a girl-friended Sam.

"Okay, okay, I won't ask anyone tonight. I'll come back with Special Kay in a few days without you and find out then." This caused raised eye-brows and attempted protests from Kay that were quickly quelled by Naughty, who determined to carry out her new mission.

I agreed on her compromise and stayed home, thoroughly mortified by her plan, yet impatient about learning her findings. Actually, part of me almost didn't want to know; I was quite happy living in my little Mexican dream world. He couldn't have a girlfriend. It was obvious that he equally adored me . . . *right?*

The next day I checked in for their report.

"So, we managed to talk to someone."

"You didn't mention *me*, did you?" I would never be able to go back in there if Sam found out.

"Well, we sat down at a discreet table and ordered some drinks. As soon as we felt it was safe, we stopped a waitress. I said that I had 'a friend' who thought Sam was cute and was wondering if he happened to be single. Since I was with Special Kay, the waitress probably thought she was 'the friend'!"

Poor Special Kay—she didn't deserve to get pulled into this. She was highly selective when it came to men; I doubted she would be caught dead dating a bartender, even if he was absolutely to die for. Kay was looking for a sweet Frenchman to marry, yet she kept going out with her boss's evil son, hence her current bitterness and weariness towards *man*kind.

"And so . . .?" Even if I was against her tactics, I couldn't hold out any longer.

"She didn't know a Sam! They don't have a Sam working there!"

"What do you mean?" I asked, baffled.

"His name isn't Sam . . . it's *Julio!*"

Julio? It seemed that I needed to get my hearing checked. Well, at least Julio made more sense for a Mexican name than Sam. And Julio was much more fitting for a ravenous lover's name. How tempting and exciting: *Julllllio.*

I came back down to earth and to the *real* question at hand: "And so . . . did she know if *Julio* has a girlfriend?"

"Well, once we got the name settled and she realized who we were asking about, she confirmed that he indeed has a girlfriend."

My heart sank deep, deep, down into the bottom of my chest. That was **not** good news. I'd been totally convinced that he was supposed to be my summer fling. Fate had handed him to me on a silver platter . . . well, more like a beer tray. Or rather not at all—I'd been deceived by destiny! *Woe was totally me!* But wait a second! I couldn't give up just like that. What did this waitress know? Maybe she'd gotten confused over the purported Sam aka Julio and just said whatever came to mind. That was possible . . . *right?* Or maybe *she* had a secret crush on Julio and wanted to stave off any possible female threats? Yes, that was more like it. The girl was clearly completely untrustworthy.

I would not and could not lose hope. We all agreed that he flirted much more with me than he should if he really had a girlfriend; and, he gave me far more attention than any other girl in that bar.

One Friday night, I went to the pub with a few of the girls. It wasn't such a busy night so I got a chance to chat up Julio. Too much time had gone by since our doomed flirting had begun. Summer was nearing and I needed to get my fling started! I had to make my move that night. Another Cosmo would help.

While he was preparing my drink, our conversation got a little heated, and I wasn't the only one throwing logs on the fire!

"So, Julio, when's your next concert? I would love to hear you perform again," I pitched.

"Well, we aren't really a band, but I hope to play again soon. Or else, I'm available for private performances . . ."

"Oh, really? What *kind* of performances?"

"Well, I could dance, if someone would sing for me . . ."

he said, with a sly little smile.

"I'm not a very good singer, but I *am* a good dancer and I could also be a very good audience. When can I arrange a private show?" I dared, leaning closer to him over the bar, inches from his succulent lips.

"Any time you want," he proposed, staring me straight in the eyes. *Wow, hot stuff. I was absolutely, divinely melting! A private dance with Julio?* Locked with Julio in a shared gaze, I turned the *risqué* level up a notch.

"Is that so? How about after work . . . tonight?" I couldn't believe I'd just said that . . . and I think he couldn't either. We were frozen in an intense moment, painfully shattered by a drink request from the other end of the bar.

I can be remarkably daring when the occasion calls, which it has a few times in my life. Tonight was about to make its way onto that list. Time was ticking by and the girls wanted to leave to catch the last *métro* home. I had to act—it was now or (*maybe*) never. I grabbed our drink bill, turned it over and scribbled down my number as Julio was coming back over.

"When you finish work, I'd love to take you up on that dance offer." And with that I slid the precious piece of paper across the bar. He picked it up and had a look. Now it was his turn to blush.

"Hope to see you later," I said, with my own sly little smile as I turned towards the door.

Had I really just given him my number? On my way home to the northern steeps of Montmartre, I was both extremely nervous and on an incredible high. *Was he going to call? Had I shaved my legs that morning? Was I wearing sexy underwear?*

That was the first time I'd offered out my number without being asked for it . . . and it would **be the last**. Once home,

I stayed up for a good hour or so fretting, awaiting his call—however, my phone lay silent. Nor did he call in the nights or weeks that followed. My hopes were utterly and irrevocably dashed. I'd gotten it wrong—*but how?* What had happened to fate? Could it be possible that Julio didn't like me after all?

Sadly, I had to accept that Julio was not meant to be my summer fling. There would be no declarations of *je t'aime*, or in this case, *ti amo*. I would eventually, *somehow*, get over him. I hated to admit it, but Naughty was right; I had to stay away from bar boys; that was surely the problem. Though slightly depressed, I couldn't let this little defeat get me down—I merely had to come up with some good resolutions to help me find an even **better** candidate for my summer fling. But, the question remained: could I find another *petit dieu* with as much sexy godliness as my little Mayan God of Music?

DAVE [05/13/05 7:52 PM]
Care to meet up at the Rendez-vous
for a drink? Would love to see you.

Summer Fling Resolutions – May

- Stay away from sexy bartenders (or maybe just Mexican ones?)

    - or maybe more globally, stay away from bar-boys altogether

    - or even bars (nah, too restrictive, perhaps just Canadian bars?)

- Don't fall under spell of sexy charm (so hard not to!— this will be a tough one)

- Don't disregard carefully-obtained information such as "Yes, he has a girlfriend"

- If potential candidate has a girlfriend (don't waste so much time next time!)

- Don't blindly believe in fate!

- Don't <u>give out</u> phone number before being asked for

MUY CALIENTE?

BOBBIE [05/22/05 1:24 PM]
Hola Guapa. I hope your Saturday was good! I'm doing fine, well rested! I hope to see you as soon as you have time in your busy schedule! Kisses

"I don't think we should be doing this . . ." uttered a faint voice from the back seat.

"Don't worry, we'll be fine. Besides, the two of us could take him, hands down," I whispered back.

Do you remember what your mother always told you when you were a kid? Never talk to strangers, never take candy from them (did free drinks fall into this category?), and above all, never ever get into strangers' cars (did "never go home with them" come after this?).

I gave Naughty a reassuring smile. For now, we'd only broken the first and third rules. Here we were in a slightly beat-up little red car, zooming through the empty Paris streets as dawn was slowly waking up some people, and putting others, ourselves included, to bed. To bed . . . *but where?*

"Come on, *pleeease* . . . we take your friend home and I make you breakfast at my place," pleaded our Spanish drier, one hand on my leg, one hand on the steering wheel, eyes wavering dangerously in between.

I shot a somewhat less reassuring glance back at panic-stricken Naughty. How did we end up in this mess? How had our mothers' concerned advice slipped our minds? A long night and numerous Mojitos were certainly to blame!

Saturday night had rolled around and Naughty and I were out loose on our own. Naughty never missed a chance to go dancing, and as Special Kay (who, like her taste in men, was also more selective with her music styles) had other plans for the evening, salsa dancing was the first suggestion on Naughty's lips. *Por qué no?* I hadn't been salsa dancing, and in particular back to *La Piñata*, since Kay and I had gone out there a few Halloweens ago. On that occasion, another random Spanish-speaking *chico* had tried to tempt me with his "breakfast menu." This one was not so difficult to turn down, given that he was sporting a plastic witch-hat-and-hair combo as a costume. On the other hand, *La Piñata* was only a few streets away from *The Reindeer*, and thus a stone's throw from memories of Julio . . . perhaps this night would give me a chance to find a new *corazón*.

My spirits instantly perked up with the fiesta energy of *La Piñata*; the lively Latino rhythms blasting through the air summoned us to the dance floor. Salsa imperatively involves dancing with a partner, usually of the opposite sex, so we'd spent the night swapping overly sweaty, overly friendly dance partners until one overstayed his one-dance quota. This was Bobbie from Madrid. I immediately wondered where on earth he got such an oddly un-Spanish name. Was it a nickname? My querying was the result of my past mix-up over Sam/Julio. A later glance at his passport proved that this was indeed his real first name—his parents must have taken some good drugs back in the seventies or else were extremely fond of the English language.

Had I found a real Latin lover this time? Was I just trying to make up for the Julio upset? Julio was pretty hard to replace. Granted, if I were a reasonable person, I might have stayed away from all Spanish-speaking *hombres* after my last experience, but that wasn't really fair. I couldn't let Julio give them *all* a bad name either. Maybe Bobbie would be different.

Back on the *caliente* dance floor, I had managed to engage in a little conversation with him. It turned out that he'd been working in Paris for a few years, was about my age, and liked dancing . . . *hmmm, maybe he was worth a try?* He was rather cute, friendly and had a terribly sexy accent. And, to his credit, up to that point, he hadn't put on any sly moves.

As the night was rapidly becoming morning, Naughty and I decided it was time to leave the club. Bobbie said that he had a car and with true Spanish chivalry, offered to drive us home. Finding a taxi at that hour in Paris was always a daunting task, so we accepted his invitation. It seemed like a good idea at first—that was, until we were en route and he began insistently begging me to go home with him. Naughty's roommate was away for the weekend and we'd planned to have a sleepover at her place. As it was, we would have to make do with the few hours we had left of the night/morning and it was out of the question that I ditch her for some *chico* I'd just met (unless he'd been Julio's twin brother, of course).

"*Pleeease* . . . I make a good breakfast. I get fresh croissants at the bakery. Do you prefer tea or coffee . . .?"

"But she can't!" piped up Naughty. "We are both having lunch tomorrow with my . . . aunt. She's in Paris only for the, *umm*, the weekend and she's expecting us promptly at . . . ten."

Good one, Naughty. Now we just had to make the story believable and stick to it.

"Yes, I love her aunt. It's so great that she's in Paris," I added. "She would be really disappointed if we, I mean, *I* didn't go for lunch. You see, she rarely comes to visit and I haven't seen her in a really long time." *More like never before in my entire life—so I wasn't really lying then, was I?*

"But I can take you there . . . *after* breakfast," rebutted Bobbie, trying to seal the deal with his cutest smile.

"Oh, I wouldn't want to trouble you. She lives—I mean she's *staying*—right near Naughty's place. And it's very, very far from where you live," I continued. Would that be enough to subdue him?

"It's more than near—she's staying in the same building!" tacked on Naughty. Okay, maybe our story was getting a little far-fetched.

"But it's too sad to end such a wonderful evening . . ." he declared, caressing my cheek.

"She **HAS** to come with me!" cried Naughty, reaching a new level of panic.

"She's right. I really must go. But we can have breakfast another time," I promised, hoping that this would finally satisfy him.

Luckily, we were nearing Naughty's building in the posh 16th *arrondissement* of Paris, which was still soundly asleep (at least until Bobbie's rattling car had noisily raced by). Only a few more of these snooty streets left to hold him off.

"It's so nice of you to drive us home," I thanked him sweetly.

"Yes, my aunt will be happy to know we made it back safely. You can drop us off right here!" ordered Naughty, her stress level reaching its ultimate height.

With numbers exchanged and a quick kiss goodbye, we jumped out of his dingy, double-parked car, trying to avoid smacking the door into the adjacent row of neatly parked Mercedes and BMWs. We scurried inside, praising Naughty's good aunt who'd saved the day—or rather, helped us with our early morning escape from Breakfast with Bobbie.

After an all-too-brief sleep, Naughty and I groggily crawled out of bed for our aunt-less, Bobbie-less brunch on the sunny terrace. There, I had the whole city before me. The lazy Seine River, lined with its docked *péniche* houseboats, and peppered with touristy *bateaux-mouches*. Beyond them lay the imposing *la Grande Dame de Paris*: the Eiffel Tower. Further afield, we could glimpse the shiny dome of Les Invalides, and further off into the distance, the snowy dome of Sacré Cœur Basilica crowning Montmartre. The glistening city looked so perfect; I wished my mind could have reflected this same glorious peaceful state.

"Naughty, I don't know if I really want to see this guy again or not." There it was—my inevitable indecisiveness surfacing.

"Well, he did seem pretty clingy. I'd watch out for that. But at least he's not a bartender, and he *is* a good dancer . . ." This latter factor granted him an automatic first approval from Naughty. *Hmmm . . . what did I have to lose?* He might turn out to be a really great guy, and the perfect little pick-me-up summer fling that I was looking for. He wasn't as incredibly sexy as Julio, but maybe that was part of Julio's problem: he was just too darn adorable for his (and my) own good.

BOBBIE [05/17/05 8:43 PM]

**Free for a Spanish dinner
one of these nights?**

Bobbie had kindly offered to make me an authentic Spanish dinner, an invitation I really couldn't refuse. By sending me a message within two days, and trying to invite me to dinner instead of skipping straight to the whole breakfast thing again, he earned some major points!

However, in focusing on these positive points, I naively skipped over one major factor that would later surface—during our date.

We decided on the following Friday night, the best option in spite of the fact that I had to teach at the University the next morning. On the other hand, my class could provide me with a good excuse to make it an early night.

BOBBIE [05/18/05 9:33 PM]

**Great! You don't need bring
anything. Just your pretty
blonde self! A vendredi!**

Ahhh, flattery! That immediately won him some more points. But upon learning where he lived, he almost lost them again. Bobbie lived in one of the sketchiest areas of Paris:

the northeast of the city. Its aging high-rise apartment blocks were a far cry from the picturesque postcard Paris I'd been admiring from Naughty's balcony the previous weekend. It wasn't necessarily a dangerous place, but nonetheless, it was a district where being "your pretty blonde self" can often draw unwanted attention. While being far from an elitist, I did care about my personal safety! I decided that I would take the risk and venture into this potentially perilous territory. It couldn't be that bad, and it was for a good cause . . . *right?*

That Friday night, at precisely ten minutes after the assigned rendezvous time, I made my way up the *métro* steps under the gawking stare of the crowd of men loitering around the *métro* entrance, cat-calling or hissing at any attractive damsel exiting the station. *Yuck!* This was not the ideal way to start off my evening, but the creepy men quickly slipped out of my mind when I saw Bobbie's enthusiastic smile.

"Bonsoir ma Tigresse!" He greeted me with a smooth kiss on each cheek before rapidly whisking me away to the safe haven of his nearby second-floor abode. After a quick tour of his place and a rapid scan of his bookshelf (he scored some more points with a good collection of French and Spanish literature and no photos of possible girlfriends or children left behind in Madrid), we settled down on the sofa.

It was *apéro* time, which normally involves, oh, I don't know, something to drink such as *vino* or *cerveza*, and usually accompanied by olives, peanuts or chips . . . and don't the Spanish do tapas? It seemed that this tradition hadn't been imported by this particular Spaniard, as the only thing served for *apéro* appeared to be . . . *ME!* And Bobbie was hungry! *Hold on there . . . we hadn't even finished with the basic small talk.* I managed to remove him from my lips to ask him a few questions about himself. At that moment, remembering that he had, in fact, invited me over for dinner, Bobbie broke out some flat soda from the fridge. Where was the vodka to go with it? And the munchies?

I managed to learn a bit more about him while pretending to enjoy my deflated *eau-de-Sprite*. Time was getting on and, true to Spanish eating habits, he got up to get dinner ready around 10:30 pm. Bobbie had promised me a traditional Spanish meal. When I'd told him via text message that I was vegetarian, he had said *no problemo*—he'd make *tortilla* (in Spain, this is a thick omelet made of egg and potato). Great! That sounded yummy. I'd never had a real homemade one prepared by the loving hands of an actual Spaniard, and was looking forward to it.

From the kitchen, my cute chef sounded hard at work with the clanking of pots and pans, when he suddenly popped his head out:

"I had a busy day at work, and didn't have time to go shopping, but luckily I already had this one," Bobbie proudly declared, showing off a packaged *tortilla* from the local discount supermarket. Points were rapidly plummeting from his previously adequate score.

"I also forgot to get some wine, but very luckily again, I have some left from a few nights ago."

WHAT? Pre-made tortilla and *left-over wine?* Those offerings certainly didn't pass, especially considering that there was a nice, big, *fancy* supermarket right across the street from his place. He must have had a siesta or two during a few crucial classes of "Dating 101" and "Wining and Dining 202." Not wanting to be too snobbish, I smiled and shrugged it off. Besides, my grumbling stomach and increasing doubts about this guy called for an immediate remedy—days-old wine would have to do. We finished our tortilla and green salad (i.e., lettuce), talking about a variety of mediocre subjects. He cleared our plates and came back only with his big smile. No dessert? No *digestivo? Nada?* Once again, I brushed it off; maybe he was just not much of a cook . . . or host . . . or out to impress me at all.

We retired to the sofa. After we had managed to talk for a few minutes, he pulled his Latin lover card again, stronger than before. If he had impressed me with dinner, he probably would have had more instant luck, but he had lost most of his good points and would have to work hard to get them back. Talk or flattery would have to come first. Detaching the lip-suction, I got his lips moving in another way.

"So, what are your life's ambitions?" I was hoping to spark up conversation by asking him stupid questions, but only had the time to ask two before he attacked me again. Struggling to back him off, I had to pull out all the stops.

"Bobbie, this is a little much for me. You see, my last boyfriend was so unaffectionate, I need a little space."

"But I'm Spanish! I can't help myself—this is the way I am!"

We can't very well change our genetic make-up, now, can we? I'm not sure if passion is found in DNA, though. Maybe it is. Or maybe we northerners just can't bear being smothered by kisses from someone we barely know?

Somehow, the clock was dangerously ticking towards 1:00 am and I had just missed the *métro.* This was when I realized my mistake . . . *What had I been thinking?* Apparently I hadn't been thinking at all. Dating rule #15: Don't be lured into having a first real date at either person's home. This will inevitably lead to TROUBLE.

Unfortunately, I would only start applying this vital rule after a few more dating mishaps.

Bobbie was trying to coax me into staying for "a little longer," a vague time frame that would inevitably meld into "all night," and I did have to work the next morning. For two years (I'd started at the university just after the art gallery job flop), I'd been trudging out to the suburbs (quite similar in appearance to Bobbie's neighborhood) two nights a week and every Saturday morning to teach English conversation classes at a university. On the surface, it was a rather easy, well-paid gig. Yet, it came with a few downsides—location, schedule, was and worst of all, the sleazy program director. I was pretty sure that he'd hired me for my looks rather than my credentials; however, this was during my poorest époque in Paris, when I was reduced to selling off most of my books for rent money, and forced into eating discount supermarket pasta with olive oil. Obviously in a state of desperation, I tried my best to ignore his inappropriate comments and ogling (sexual harassment workplace policies aren't strictly enforced in France—or maybe they don't even exist?).

It was clear that my better judgment mechanisms had malfunctioned earlier on in the evening (like when I had agreed to come over in the first place), leaving me to choose between Plan A (risking my life outdoors while trying to hail a taxi in what could easily be referred to as a Parisian ghetto), or the far more terrifying Plan B (staying over). Even though he was too affectionate, it was kind of nice to have at least a little attention. It was certainly better than what I'd been used to with Stéphane, that being pretty much none at all! Or was it better? I obviously wasn't totally into him or I would have been a little more receptive. But what about my summer fling? I was looking for someone fun and easy-going, after all. It only had to last the summer. Did I have to be so picky? He was definitely very, very passionate and very into me (perhaps his admiration had clouded his social etiquette earlier in the evening?). Maybe I should just go with the flow and give him a try. The consequences would have to be dealt with later.

"I drive you to work in the morning. *Stayyyyy*," was his plea of a few hours prior. And my final response had been "Okay." In the end, it was a bad idea; with all that passion of his, he barely let me sleep a wink. And, after all that, I fully realized that I wasn't into him and highly doubted that he was my summer fling candidate. He, however, continued to become more and more attached to me.

At 8:00 am, the Parisian roads were still very empty, reminiscent of our previous early morning drive when I'd refused his breakfast invite. This time I got my tea and croissant, but I wasn't sure that they'd been entirely worth it. *Ugggh.* Teaching was going to be rough; maybe I could put a movie on for my students, or perhaps they could do some independent reading or something while I took a wee little nap?

"You can drop me off at the lights," I instructed as we were approaching the campus. The last thing I needed was for one of my adoring colleagues or the slimy school director to see me with Bobbie (actually, that might have been a good thing; they might have left me alone if they thought I had a new boyfriend).

"Good luck with your class, my *Tigresse*." And with that he managed to get a little good-bye kiss as I leapt out of his rolling car.

After making it through the relatively painless lesson—helped along by some dreadfully grim, but absolutely necessary coffee—I hurried home as fast as I could and hopped into my nice, *empty* bed. I was already in a deep sleep when his cute message arrived.

> **BOBBIE [05/22/05 1:24 PM]**
> Hola Guapa. I hope your Saturday was good! I'm doing fine, well rested! I hope to see you as soon as you have time in your busy schedule! Kisses

Would my busy schedule have any time for him . . .? *Jeez*, that required some serious contemplation . . .

This all happened at a stage in my dating life before I'd realized that there wasn't any point in torturing myself with seeing someone more than once, even when the attraction vibes weren't there. But as I was freshly back on the dating scene, eagerly seeking my summer fling candidate (and also being incredibly indecisive), I decided to give him one more chance. And, I wouldn't confess to the girls that I'd stayed over on Friday—I'd be in for a lynching.

Somehow we met back at his place (it obviously takes me a while to learn my lesson!). However, this time I'd come armed with conviction: I was going to stay strong and I was not going to stay long.

I think Bobbie could tell that I was a little distant and less receptive than before, so he gave it his all. He was also armed with his own conviction mission, which was to passionately seduce me, with no holds barred! And he wasn't serving up flat soda this time . . . the only items on the menu seemed to be Latin love kisses!

Okay, I give up! I don't want a Latin lover! What had I been thinking? Truce! Truce! Or rather, S.O.S.! Or whatever it is in Spanish—*Ayudame!* I had to escape, but unfortunately for me, Naughty's aunt couldn't save me this time.

"I have to go! Now!" I desperately screeched. I'd successfully pushed him off for a long enough air break to tell him that I wasn't ready to get all passionate, and that I needed some time (well, maybe a lifetime before I decided to see this *Señor Amor* again). I was expecting more over-emotional pleas to try to get me to stay. Instead, I had to give him credit for his rather unique response: he started taking off his clothes!

Okay, he only got as far as his shirt (my clothes were firmly buttoned up, though he'd tried unsuccessfully to creep up my skirt, inch-by-quick-inch).

The whole situation was becoming quite funny and it was hard to suppress my giggles.

"No, I really need to go now," I managed to declare between laughing and trying to find my jacket. Had something been lost in translation or did he think he'd win me over with his not-that-muscular, but thankfully not hairy, chest?

"Before you go, let's take some pictures," he suggested, jumping up for his camera.

"What kind of pictures?" I questioned, alarmed. The idea was a little out-of-the-blue and not exactly appropriate, seeing as he was shirtless, and I was flushed and trying to escape (wanting never to see him again, might I add).

"I just want a photo of you, *Guapa.*"

"Not now! Look at the state we're in," I rebutted, patting down my disheveled hair.

"Come on, *ma Tigresse,* just one or two . . ." he insisted in an especially puppy-dog-drooling way. Would he let me go only after surrendering to a few pictures? He didn't seem to be after any sexy, risqué images, so . . . what the heck? By this point, I was pretty sure that I wasn't going to return his calls, so I thought it better to appease him in the interest of pulling a quick disappearing act.

"*Queso!*" I struck a cheesy pose, putting on my best fake smile—it may have even looked genuine, thanks to thoughts of me being safe, sound and *alone* at home.

"Now you take one of me," he said.

"Well, if you insist." It would make a funny souvenir. I pulled out my phone and snapped a shot of the shirtless, seductive-less Spaniard (an anomaly indeed!).

"You're not really leaving, are you?" he whimpered, trying to tempt me to stay by smattering his little kisses up and down my arm. That was the wrong type of temptation; a triple vodka on the rocks or strongly spiked sangria might have worked, but I wasn't about to give him any useful pointers.

"Yes, I have to go, but maybe we could get a drink next week?" Famous last words, but somehow they still worked.

"Okay, I hope to see you soon."

"Sure, *hasta la vista!*" *Or not!* With that *adios*, I escaped from the sketchy streets of the 19th back to my safe abode in Montmartre.

BOBBIE [06/01/05 7:26 PM]

Hola Guapa! How about getting
that drink you suggested?

Okay, perhaps I didn't really want a Latin lover. They were actually a bit intense and way too . . . *picanté!* Or at least Bobbie was. Maybe that was a little too much *je t'aime/ti amo* for me. Where was my quest taking me? For the time being, I hadn't been heading down the right *calle* or the right *rue* for that matter. After this second blunder, it seemed this wasn't going to be as easy as I'd thought. Maybe making some new resolutions would help? In any case, I wasn't going to give up looking for my *aventure*; I really did want my pick-me-up fling and the summer was officially about to begin. There had to be other reasonable catches out there.

So I recast my fishing line . . .

♥

ENRICO [06/02/05 9:51 PM]

Have I told you lately that you're
beautiful? Can't wait to see
you, my dear! xoxo

DAVE [06/06/05 7:43 PM]
How about a drink?

"What's wrong with a little affection?"

"He was suffocating me!"

"He was just a passionate guy, and you deprived him, the poor thing," teased Dave.

"The 'poor thing'? If he'd had his way, I'd probably be locked up in his apartment right now as his love-slave/personal chef! He certainly needed some help in that latter domain—definitely not the former." How could he actually be defending Bobbie?

"You could have really helped him out. You're cruel."

"So now I'm the mean one! It was Bobbie who practically starved me!"

"I thought you were looking for a little summer loving?"

"Yes, the key word there being: little."

"I know where you can get a little loving . . . " he said slyly as he set his hand on the table, not far from mine.

Yikes! I flung my hand into the air, frantically flagging down the waiter for our bill—it was time to get out of there . . . while I still could!

Summer Fling Resolutions - June

- Stay away from bar boys (!)
- Or bars (especially ~~Canadian~~ foreign-themed bars—i.e. Salsa bars)
- Be wary of Spanish-speaking boys (both from Spain _and_ any ex-colonies)
- Don't accept car rides home/to work (even if the invitation comes from the owner of a Mercedes, Porsche, Ferrari . . . wellll . . . would have to reconsider this resolution should the 'luxury car' occasion arise)
- Don't accept invitations to dinner at **his** place on the first date (no matter which district he lives in!)
- Suss out dinner preparation skills (again, not for the first date, but for an eventual third or fourth date)
- Don't give a guy you think you're not into a second chance! . . . May end up as kidnapped love slave next time!
- Try to gauge level of passion . . . not too much, not too little

AND: Be wary of Dave's advice!

A ROLL IN THE HAY

JULIEN [06/22/05 5:28 PM]
I'm dying to see you again!
Let's pick up where we left off!

Where am I? Who am I with? More importantly . . . who am I kissing? These are not good questions to wake up asking yourself, especially when you don't know the answers! Well, from what I could immediately gather, the answer to the first question seemed to be "a wheat field," which could have been pretty much anywhere. The answers to the other two questions would remain—for the time being—something of a mystery . . .

How had I ended up in a wheat field at the crack of dawn being ferociously kissed by a young, sun-streaked blond stud? No, I wasn't on the set of the kind of racy TV show screened after midnight on French public channels. And no, I hadn't gotten lost on a hike in the country and been rescued by a shepherd boy . . . *or had I?*

The weather was finally heating up (and, so it seemed, was my love life!). Every day the thermometer crept higher and higher. Unfortunately, while Paris is very enjoyable in mild sunny weather, it can be truly unbearable in a heat wave, or in French, *la canicule*. Air conditioning is virtually non-existent, and the chilliest places in town are supermarket frozen food sections—not the "coolest" of *cool* places to hang out. *La canicule* can even be quite deadly: one a few years ago was so suffocating that it actually killed thousands of people! So when Special Kay invited me to go along with her to a colleague's country home for the weekend, I enthusiastically jumped at the chance to get out of the stifling (and potentially life-threatening) city and onto a reclining garden chair in some peaceful smog-free *jardin*, a chilled cocktail in hand *bien sûr*.

Special Kay's colleague was organizing a big party to celebrate the momentous conclusion of his second home's 20-year-long renovation. It was finally finished, and they were now considering selling the place. This seemed normal to me, though—many French people undergo similar arduous endeavors, only to sell in the end. Alas, it's a shame they can't just enjoy the fruits of their labor. Nevertheless, we were all surely going to enjoy the place at least briefly during the *fête*. And besides, Jean-Luc, though a fair amount older than us, was extremely young at heart and full of fun.

Sadly, I was working out at the university in the morning and could only join the festivities in the late afternoon. This Saturday morning would not be like the others; it was the last class of the semester and we were having an end-of-year luncheon. I was not only celebrating finishing for the semester, I was also celebrating my resignation. I'd found enough work inside Paris, so no more early trips out to the suburbs (by *métro* or by car, driven by adoring escorts), and no more advances from the creepy director. I felt as free as a bird!

I escaped the luncheon as soon as I could . . . that is, after enjoying a copious meal accompanied by numerous glasses of congratulatory champagne. As it turned out, I'd managed to get a head start on the party and thus wouldn't be too far behind the other celebrants when I arrived.

It was taking me forever to get back into Paris, and I was starting to worry that I'd miss my train, and thus, the party! Finally reaching the Montparnasse *métro* station, I still had to make my way through the endless labyrinth of underground passageways to reach the actual train station, pushing my way through the masses of other travelers heading out on their famous five-week vacations, dragging behind them caravans of luggage and kids. I arrived within a fraction of a second, jumping onto my 3:15 pm train as its departure bells were sounding.

Eventually I caught my breath, and when I was far enough away from the city, I started to relax and take in the lovely scenery. I was headed in the direction of Chartres, a town about 100 kilometers (60 miles) south of Paris, best known for its splendid medieval cathedral. The area sort of reminded me of where I grew up, not because of its architectural masterpiece (none of those in my hometown!), but for its graceful fields of swaying wheat as far as the eye can see. I would get to know those fields far better than I would have ever envisioned a little later on . . .

Special Kay and Jean-Luc had been kind enough to come pick me up at the tiny train station in the closest village to his house. On the way back to his place, I duly noted through Jean-Luc's "loose" driving that I certainly wasn't the only one who had already kick-started the party . . . for the French, having a few drinks and then taking the wheel is, sadly and dangerously, not out of the ordinary. On the other hand, I couldn't really blame him; it was already 4:00 pm, and therefore a perfectly normal time for the French to be enjoying a Saturday post-lunch *digestif* . . . or maybe even getting closer to *apéritif* time? I tightly fastened my seatbelt and off we sped along the winding, one-lane country roads.

About 20 minutes later, we arrived at our destination—in one piece and without being stopped at a roadside police check point (the cops were probably having their afternoon *sieste* anyway). I discovered that his country house really *was* in the country with no direct neighbors . . . except for some friendly-looking trees . . . and smiling chaffs of wheat. From past conversations with French friends, I'd come to realize that their "country homes" were actually in villages or towns, and not in countryside like back home, so I hadn't been expecting a *real* country cottage/farm-like residence.

As we pulled into the long driveway, I noticed a group of young people who'd created their own encampment under a large shady oak tree about halfway down the lane. *Hmmm,* it seemed like not *all* the guests would be graying. After I enquired about the youngsters, Jean-Luc told me that they were his daughter and her friends. His pretty offspring was only 17, but her good looks had charmed an "older" university boy, and it was their joint friends who made up the "counter-party." Even though Special Kay and I were technically closer in age to the younger group, we naturally spent our time with the older generation, as Jean-Luc's guests.

After a quick tour of the house, we all settled down to the business at hand: *la fête*. As it was late June, the days were still very long and the hot afternoon thus slowly ticked by, accompanied well by a constant stream of refreshing drinks. There really wasn't much else to do, but we all seemed quite content with our inactivity. I certainly hadn't come to the party looking to pick up (tasty frozen daiquiris notwithstanding!) so I was free to have a silly old time amongst these friendly old(er) revelers.

Night was gradually veiling the expansive country sky and the cocktails had morphed into wine over a barbecue-esque meal. Avoiding the gigantic pig roasting on a spit, I tracked down some salad and cheese to complement my *rosé*. Everyone was indeed *looking* rather rosy, and it wasn't only due to the blazing fire. By this time (vaguely post-dinner), Jean-Luc seemed to have already polished off two bottles of vodka without anyone's help and was trying to get a sing-along started. His English vocabulary consisted primarily of "Hello" and "Thank you," so unfortunately he wasn't the best troubadour of English songs. I sang along to a few good ones, but as neither of us could hold a tune, our duet was quickly silenced. Luckily for everyone's sake (and ears), a serious party-goer had brought his personal DJ equipment, including loud speakers and laser lights, for the full "country party" effect.

After overcoming some technical difficulties, we soon had the hottest disco between Paris and Chartres, admittedly not such a hard feat considering the lack of competition . . . This wasn't exactly the exciting Parisian night scene that we were used to in the big city, but Kay and I had to look on the bright side. Jean-Luc's living room-cum-dance floor was much less crowded than a Parisian club; with a total of 15 dancers, we had all the space we wanted. Plus, there was no chance of being hounded by the slimy wannabe suitors that were our usual burden. Somehow, the gray-haired revelers hadn't managed to tempt any of the kids to join the happening indoor party, but we didn't need them to have fun—we had wine: the secret ingredient for any good party!

The hours flew by and dancers gradually started turning in, causing our disco to start winding down. The few left standing, with any energy, packed up the equipment in order to transform our living room/dance floor into an open *auberge*. I'd lost track of Kay right around the time that Jean-Luc had collapsed face-first onto one of the outdoor picnic tables, a half-finished whiskey bottle in his hand. I assumed Kay had gone off to snooze discreetly in a corner—one of her trademark habits after a few drinks too many. As for myself, having been up for over 20 hours, and having consumed at least that many drinks, fatigue was inching over me as well. I thought it might be a nice idea to have a seat on the sofa while they finished making up the beds . . .

Making up the beds? This is where I regained consciousness in a rather unconventional sort of bed—the infamous wheat field with the sexy flockless shepherd boy (well, at least I didn't see any sheep in the vicinity or hear any bleating).

"What's your name again?" I might have been asking him this for the first time.

"Julien," he replied, and went back to savagely kissing me. Boy, he was cute—but was he 17 like Jean-Luc's daughter?

"How old are you, Julien?"

". . . *Ahhh* . . . Twenty-four . . . and you?"

"A little older than that." Yikes, that was a bit young,

but not completely out of reach.

"Age doesn't matter," he declared, shutting me up with more kisses. More famous last words . . .

Have you ever had a roll in the hay? This is normally done in a barn, with dry, cut hay that looks all fluffy and soft. However, we were not in a hay barn, but a real wheat field, and wheat is actually quite stiff and scratchy. It certainly isn't the best for having a roll in, especially when wearing a short skirt over bare legs.

Julien was getting a little too excited, and as my better judgment had returned, I firmly suggested that we go back inside. He wasn't too keen on the idea, but I was already stumbling up to a standing position to assess our location, which turned out to be only 20 or so feet from the house.

Once inside, we rummaged around for any remaining sleeping materials, finally settling on a few couch cushions and a tiny blanket, and curled up together on the floor for a few hours of attempted shuteye.

When the house started stirring and most people seemed to be getting up, we eventually had to follow suit. Julien timidly crept back to his group and I stayed with the adults, trying to act like nothing had happened. Maybe no one had really seen us together? *Just maybe?* Everyone was hung over and pretty spacey as it was.

Kay and I sat dozing in the sun for a few more hours, not doing much except for mustering up enough energy for a snail-paced stroll down the country road and back. As people started to depart, Julien reappeared. We had a little chat and he got up enough nerve to ask me for my phone number. Well, *pourquoi pas?* I knew nothing about him beyond his name . . . and that he was *très* passionate yet, from what

I sensed, much more manageable than Bobbie.

"So what's up with you and the kid?" questioned Special Kay, eyeing my hay-dotted hair.

"To tell you the truth, I'm not really sure! He saw me falling asleep on the sofa last night and thought I shouldn't be sleeping alone . . .?" I hypothesized with my very vague memory. "I think he's still a student, though. He said he was twenty-four," I added for good measure before she could comment on his youthful appearance.

"Is he an *agriculture* student?" she asked with a wink. "I only ask because, well, you have all kinds of hay in your hair." I blushed. Maybe our roll in the wheat field hadn't gone unnoticed after all.

"Did he get your number? Are you going to see him?" she prodded.

"Yes, well . . . I'm not sure . . ."

I certainly hadn't come to the country party expecting to meet my potential summer fling—but hey, sometimes the best things arrive when we least expect. The official start of summer was only days away; I needed to get my fling going before it was too late! He was also *très beau* and had a nice, sexy build to boot. I normally wasn't into blonds, but maybe Julien's carefree *jeunesse* would be just what the doctor ordered.

JULIEN [06/22/05 5:28 PM]
I'm dying to see you!
Let's pick up where we left off!

His text message arrived a few days after the party and, after a few back-and-forth messages, we set a date for the following Friday night. I wasn't sure how our night would go, but I was up for any pleasant surprises. We rendezvoused outside my *métro* entrance. I got there a little early so I wouldn't miss him (having only met him once, it might be have been tricky for me to recognize him).

"*Bonsoir*, Lily!" cheerfully greeted my sexy shepherd. *Ahhh, he's totally adorable,* I thought as he leant down to give me a peck on each cheek.

Knowing that Julien was on a student budget, I had the dilemma of choosing an appropriate restaurant. Choices, choices: a cool neighborhood hangout, or the hottest new bistro? Alas, I didn't want him to break the bank on our first date and potentially scare him off. So we ended up at a little hole-in-the-wall *crêperie*; it would be tasty, and 100 % *pas cher*. With our main course of *galette-crêpes* served up, we started to get to know each other a little better. While I wasn't too happy that Julien was still a student, learning that he was studying architecture and was, thus, on the creative side, earned him some good points. I also found out that he was from a village in the Pyrénées mountains (which meant, to me, real shepherd boy material). Coming from the southwest of France, he had this distinctively cute accent to add to his charm. Perhaps he would actually be a good fit for my summer *amour*?

The dinner flew by rapidly with our lively get-to-know-you chatter, and we finished up our *caramel beurre salée* delights and got the bill. Normally in gallant France, *le garçon* usually pays for the first date—but poor little Julien was surely living on a meager student budget so I felt obliged to chip in. Oh well, if he didn't have much money, I could be spoiled in other ways.

It was still relatively early, so I invited *petit* Julien back to my place for an after-dinner drink. I knew that this might not have been the best of ideas, but being much more experienced than him, I felt confident that I could handle any potential advances. Besides, if we had gone to a bar, I would have probably ended up paying for the drinks anyway, so why not enjoy some free ones at home?

Julien was very impressed with the exceptional view from my apartment. I left him to be enchanted while I served us up two shots of South African Amarula Cream liqueur. Standing at the edge of my windowsill, gazing out at the city, conversation turned to our summer plans.

"I'll be in Paris most of the summer. How about you?" I inquired, sizing up his summer fling potential. This was when the first of the bad news hit.

"I'm actually going down to my parents' house for the holidays." *What? Parents' house for the holidays? Drat!*

"When are you leaving?" I forced myself to ask.

"I'm finishing up my internship and heading south in about two weeks." *Drat!*

"When are you coming back?" I whimpered.

"Sometime in mid-September, just before school starts again." I did a quick calculation . . . mid-July to mid-September . . . summer would technically be over by the time he came back. There was no way he could be my summer fling! Instead of allowing myself to wallow in dismay, I decided that we could at least enjoy the rest of the evening and if I didn't find a summer fling before he got back in September, then perhaps we could go out again . . . and have an autumn fling?

This bad news called for another drink. Some spicy Gold

Strike perhaps? Its cheerful golden flecks would help me forget my romantic misery for the time being. With my yummy new drink improving my spirits, Julien pulled out his wallet to show me his student ID card with an older photo of him with very short hair (it was currently a little long and he had it tied back in a ponytail, 18th-Century shepherd boy-style). *Ahhh,* I marveled at the terribly sexy photo . . . he was such a cutie. But, as I was admiring his mountain godliness, my eyes happened to wander over to the text beside the photo:

Paris School of Architecture
Student 2005
Date of Birth: 12 January 1985

My eyes froze on that last piece of information . . . 1985 . . . I did some more quick math. "Julien, are you really *just twenty?* In the country you told me you were twenty-four!"

"Oh, did I? Well, I'm going to be twenty-one in January."

"Julien, I'm going to be twenty-seven in a month!"

"Is that a problem?" he asked innocently. *Was that a problem?* Of course it was a problem! It was for me, anyway. He had seemed so young and naive . . . because he really *was* young and naive! I tried explaining that it would not be possible for us to start dating. We were from different worlds; he needed to live a full and fun student life and I was a semi-adult with different perspectives. True, I wasn't looking for Mr. Serious right now, but I doubted that there was even any point in thinking of having an "autumn fling" with Julien *le jeune.* Notwithstanding his young age, I also needed someone who was going to physically *be* in Paris—it would be rather difficult to have a long distance "fling." Hopefully going back to the drawing board wouldn't be like looking for a needle in a haystack; I'd had enough trouble with the latter.

This additional bad news definitely called for yet another drink, specifically something nice and strong. I poured us two tall shots of a mysterious home-brewed *eau de vie* liqueur that I'd excavated from the back of the shelf. We stood for a while, leaning against the window railing, giggling at silly jokes; these harmless flirtations were accompanied by spying on the neighbors across the street, as well as the bar-goers overflowing from the boisterous *Chez François*.

As I was getting rather tipsy from all the pick-me-ups, I'd pretty much forgotten this new roadblock in my quest to find a summer lover, and any thoughts of *je t'aime*-ing were distancing themselves from my foggy mind. I looked into my empty shot glass and then over at Julien, whose eyes might have had an extra starlight (or liqueur-ed) twinkle to them. They, and the sparkling city, beckoned with possibility.

"Well it's almost time for you to catch the *métro*. Oh Julien, what am I ever going to do with you . . .?"

♥

HANS [06/25/05 9:37 PM]
When can I see you?

DAVE [06/26/05 7:49 PM]
Wish you were here.

"What's wrong with dating someone younger?"

"He's not just a little younger . . . he's practically a child!"

"That's ageist. You shouldn't care so much about age; it should be what's inside that counts." *Easier said than done.* This sort of talk wasn't surprising coming from Dave. "He probably has many great qualities: youth, vitality, endurance?"

"He certainly had all of *those* characteristics. I could use someone just a tad more mature."

"Oh, really? Is that so?" His interest was suddenly piqued as he gently put his hand on the table.

"Let's not talk about this anymore. There's no point anyway—he'll be gone in a matter of days."

"Fair enough. If he'll be away for the summer, then that's that. You may have to settle for someone a little closer . . . to home?" His sentence trailed out, and his hand inched not-so-discreetly across the table.

I quickly picked up my wine glass and took a big gulp, trying to divert his inevitable attempt to grab my hand. It was certainly time to head home. Fishing line and tackle box stowed carefully away, I was definitely not at the *Rendez-vous* to do any fishing!

Summer Fling Resolutions - July

- Be very cautious with anyone who *looks* young . . .
he probably IS

- Try to find out ASAP if potential candidate will be in
Paris over the next two months

- Don't assume a "country party" will be a "safe" event!

- (Try to) avoid consuming a number of drinks
proportionate to hours awake

- Avoid passing out in unknown territory

- Don't fall for shepherd-boy-innocent charm

- Stay away from wheat, straw, or any other similar grain-
like substance

FRENCH *CHARME*

VALENTINO [07/04/05 10:48 PM]
Bring nothing in your suitcases except your smile & your delicious voice. I'll take care of the rest. To hear you is always a pleasure, to see you will be magic . . .

—Next stop: Poitiers—

I took my little bag down from the luggage rack and gave myself a quick look over in the mirror for signs of streaked mascara or lipstick on my teeth. My heart rate stepped up a notch as I got off the train and followed the mass of descending travelers along the platform and into the station. I glanced over the waiting crowd. There didn't seem to be any sign of him. I stayed put and tried to look like I was patiently waiting. Little by little, the other passengers were enthusiastically met and whisked away by their respective friends, family members or lovers, and the crowd slowly dissipated, leaving me all by myself. *Oh dear, had I made a mistake in coming? Was I totally crazy? What was I even doing there?*

"Bonjour, ma Princesse," greeted a soft voice to my left. I swung around to find a smiling man approaching to give me a kiss—I guessed that had to be him . . .

We have to backtrack a few weeks, to what had started out as a rather "average" Saturday night. Sweet little Julien had deserted me for his shepherd boy's retreat in the Pyrénées, so I was once again on the hunt for my summer fling. Mid-July still counted as the summer! But I knew I had to get things going—and fast—or my whole plan would be a big flop.

Like many a Saturday night, *les filles* had congregated at my place to get the night started off with a good dose of *vin*, gossip and laughter. The guests comprised the usual suspects: Naughty, Special Kay and Pussycat, plus our dear friend Cindy, who sadly no longer lived in Paris, but was in town for an evening of "Girls Just Want to Have Fun."

Around midnight, Cindy began lining up shots and got us dancing around my tiny apartment. With the festive fires well-stoked, we headed across town to *Le Sous-sol*, a nice, but not-too-expensive basement club that we sometimes went to in the Latin Quarter area, a stone's throw away from Notre Dame, but hidden so as not to attract wandering tourists. The clientele was also generally a notch above some those found at the free places we found ourselves at. That didn't mean the guys there didn't try their best to pick us up; they were just better dressed and more tactful about it.

Cindy kept the F.U.N. barometer on the rise and we danced up a storm. Earlier in the evening, I had kind of been hoping that I might run or *dance* into a cute fling candidate, but there were slim pickings on the dance floor. It didn't really matter; I was really there to be with the girls. I could find my fling another night.

Rather late into the evening, two guys started dancing next to us. I thought that they might try to move in on us; however, they seemed totally oblivious to the group of pretty girls right next to them, and were instead having a rather sexy dance with . . . each other. Their dance became increasingly racy and, as a result, we assumed they were a couple. So when one of them started dancing close to me, thinking he must be gay, I thus played along with his friendly dance routine. It would be harmless to dance with him; he really didn't appear to be into girls. Eventually, we started talking a bit; he introduced himself as Valentino and he told me that he was Italian. I naturally broke out my Italian, asking where he was from, only to be met with a dumbstruck look. Okay, he was a little less Italian than he fashioned himself to be; he was just a drunk Italian descendant. That really didn't matter—I was already fascinated by this mysterious stranger.

Valentino and his group had a table to themselves so the two of us sat down for a break from the dance floor. As our conversation expanded, I discovered that the other guy was in fact his brother, not his lover . . . *Hmmm*, I knew Italians were generally very close-knit, but not usually *that* close. So, a few things were clearer now: he wasn't gay, I was drinking his rum and Coke . . . and I was now trapped on the inside of his table. *Uh-oh.* Had I gotten myself into a little bit of a bind? I sized him up. He didn't look too dangerous, nor did he have any darkly-clad Mafioso-looking friends with him. I figured I should be able to survive sitting there without being kidnapped or attacked by kisses.

I gathered that he'd had quite a few of those rum and Cokes, bringing out a good sense of humor but a lot of nonsense, too. I liked quirky guys; maybe tonight would actually be productive for my summer fling quest? He also seemed older than 20 and, in this low lighting, he seemed cute enough . . . so he passed the preliminary test.

After a while, Cindy managed to track me down and I could tell it was time to venture home. I started my goodbyes and was trailed to the exit by my newfound friend.

"I'm only in town until Monday morning—can I see you tomorrow?" he pleaded.

"I can't, I already have plans." I wasn't even making up excuses this time. Kay and I had reserved the afternoon to go to an art exhibit, and I wasn't about to ditch her for some potentially incestuous (though intriguing) Romeo.

"But I'll be leaving after that."

"Where will you be going?"

"Back to work. I work in Poitiers." *Poitiers?* Why would anyone ever want to work outside of Paris? And especially, why in Poitiers, a small city about a two-hour train ride from the capital? In all fairness, there was probably nothing wrong with Poitiers . . . nothing except the fact that it wasn't Paris! Given this new geographical information, how could Valentino possibly be my fling? This bad news practically put him as out of reach as *petit* Julien. But, wait a minute, Valentino was in Paris now and thus obviously could come up again . . . and Poitiers wasn't *that* far away (in reality, it is much closer than the Pyrénées!). Perhaps I could have a short-distance summer fling? It wasn't ideal but I was starting to get a little desperate; the summer was already a third over! While I was distracted by having to mull over these careful calculations, Valentino dove in for a little goodnight kiss. Not a bad first kiss at all; it granted him my phone number. Would that be the first and last kiss? Time would tell . . .

Slowly getting out of bed around noon the next day, I hauled myself down to meet Kay. We both were a little sleepy from the combination of the late night and drinks (I shouldn't have accepted Valentino's rum and Cokes), making it especially difficult to stifle our yawns while dragging our feet through the museum's rooms.

Beep, beep. Ah, a text message.

VALENTINO [06/28/05 2:46 PM]

My Princesse Tigresse,
please can we meet up?

Oh god—he was persistent. I threw my phone back in my purse and focused my attention on a large solid white canvas, trying to unearth some meaning.

Beep, beep.

VALENTINO [06/28/05 2:58 PM]

Even just for a coffee . . .
I have to see you.

This new message triggered a slew of dirty looks from the nearby art patrons so I promptly switched off my phone. However, the Italian stallion continued to bombard me with text messages for the rest of the afternoon, begging to see me. No, no, and NO. I wasn't going to budge, but at least the steady stream of pleading messages was entertaining. After the millionth plea, I did finally reply, apologetically declining his requests to meet up. I wasn't sure if this was normal behavior for the French or if I'd cast some sort of spell on him the night before with my good-bye kiss.

His last attempt was the best. As I hit the *open message* button I was surprised to find not another pleading request, but a photo. There he was smiling into the camera . . . shirtless. Or at least I think he was *only* shirtless—he was, after all, with his "close" brother and appeared very happy. Who knew what the two of them had been up to that afternoon? I couldn't help thinking of the same tactic pulled by the hot-to-trot Bobbie. And we know that his shirtlessness and photography skills hadn't gotten him very far. Would it work for Valentino?

Not today, anyway.

Off he went back to his little country city without succeeding in seeing me again, but the messages didn't stop with his departure. Instead, they got even more intense until, little by little, I began to eagerly await them. Then Valentino started calling me and before long our conversations had graduated from minutes to hours. He was proving himself to be a real Monsieur *Romantique*. Was this what a real Frenchman was like or was his behavior possibly accentuated by his Italian Romeo genes? Were the myths about the terribly amorous and enticing French lover actually true? Wow, maybe this was what I needed in a summer fling: someone to delicately sweep me off my feet, treat me like a *Princesse* and make me forget that I had ever been dumped.

Valentino was the director of a sort of community center and worked a lot. Thus, much to our dismay, he thought he wouldn't be able to escape to Paris for a good month. That would bring us into mid-August, much too late to start a summer fling. What could we do? His solution to this dilemma was to invite me down to Poitiers. He had a big house, a car, and even said he'd pay for my train ticket. *Hmmm* . . . it was a tempting if also somewhat risqué proposition.

"Are you sure that is such a good idea, Lily?" questioned Special Kay. Remembering his insistent behavior, she must have been a bit wary of him.

"*Ummm* . . . well, he asked so poetically," I stumbled out as I reached for the *Saint Amour* and began refilling everyone's glasses, hoping to divert their attention.

"You barely even know him," cautioned Naughty.

"Where *is* Poitiers anyway?" was Pussycat's concern. She didn't think any place beyond the strict border of the Parisian *périphérique* was worth venturing to—it was astounding that she even came to visit us up in Montmartre, which was practically at this city limit.

Oh dear, I thought, *maybe I shouldn't have told the girls.* They certainly weren't helping me make my decision, or at least an affirmative one.

"It's already July! The summer is in full swing! If I can't find a little fling in Paris, why not achieve it elsewhere? It'll be a little romantic getaway, an *aventure,*" I attempted in self-defense.

"I suppose you're right," concluded Naughty. "As you've said before . . . what's life without a bit of *aventure?*"

I was starting to win them—and myself—over with the idea.

VALENTINO [07/04/05 10:48 PM]
Bring nothing in your suitcases except your smile & your delicious voice. I'll take care of the rest. To hear you is always a pleasure, to see you will be magic . . .

It was a done deal. I would go down to visit him the following weekend. With all his romantic talk, I wasn't regretting my decision at all. I would just have to wait and see.

VALENTINO [07/07/05 12:11 AM]

48 hours before my eyes meet yours,
48 hours before my lips flutter
across yours. Sweet dreams.

And it was then that I was pulled out of my train station dream by the soft flutter of lips across my cheek.

"Hello, my *Princesse*," he greeted. "You're not disappointed, are you?"

"*Ummm* . . . of course not," I sputtered out, forcing a smile at the end. The man who'd approached me at the station was indeed the Franco-Italian romantic wordsmith. I was pretty sure his comment about being disappointed was in reference to his appearance. It was a bit of a strange thing for him to say, and it caught me off guard. Had I mustered a weird/surprised/disappointed look on my face? Had he sensed something? It was true: Valentino wasn't entirely how I'd remembered him. In the light of day, as opposed to the haze of rum and Cokes, he *did* look a little different from the picture that had remained in my mind, or for that matter, the one he'd sent me from his phone. It could be that he wasn't quite as cute as he had been in my memories, either . . . It was hard to put my finger on exactly what it was. Was it his nose, which was kind of squished in? Had it once been broken? Did that make his eyes look smaller? Something was a little off. Plus, I now realized he was actually fairly short, only a few inches taller than *petite moi*. But I'd come *allll* this way; I'd already gotten it into my mind that I'd finally found my summer fling, so in the split second I had to evaluate his question and my response, I decided to shrug off any doubts and focus on getting our weekend off to a good start.

Gentleman Valentino swung my bag over his shoulder and, hand-in-hand, we strolled around the historic center of Poitiers. Contrary to all our preemptive criticisms of it, the town was actually quite quaint, with pedestrian cobblestone streets, ancient Romanesque churches, and charming little piazzas. For a Friday night it was certainly a lot less lively than Paris, but I guess that's what you get for living in *province*. And, I hadn't come all this way to find a lively party-vibe . . . but rather some exciting passion vibes! Some drinks would certainly help spark some flames of passion, and it just so happened to be *apéro* hour, so we found ourselves a nice table on a bustling café terrace. With a strong but sweet *kir* in hand, I was soon seeing the city—and Valentino—in a whole new light! Soon I was experiencing *la vie en rose* in Poitiers. My inhibitions continued to loosen with the help of a second rosy *kir* while we looked over the dinner menu. Halfway through our meal (and our second bottle of wine), we were chatting and laughing up a storm.

I can do this! I said to myself while polishing off another glass of delicious, nerve-quelling Burgundy. Wining, dining and charming me for a few days was one way to win me over. However, Valentino had more in store as well . . . back at his place. The wine was certainly crucial in getting things going, but once the passion juices got flowing, they didn't stop until I boarded the TGV N° 6969 back to Paris on Sunday night. His intense affection and fascinating allure made up for the physical features that I was still questioning.

Overall, we had quite an exciting weekend in Poitiers . . . well, not really *in* Poitiers; after that first evening out, we spent most of the remaining time getting to know the various rooms of his house, intimately. I was on a weekend love *aventure* after all, not a cultural one. I also gradually got to discover more about Valentino, including his family, which added to his intrigue. A half-century ago back in Calabria, his grandfather had gotten into some trouble with the mafia, forcing him to flee to France. Here in exile, from what I gathered, he'd started up his own mafia branch. Well, it might have merely been a cartel on wine distribution in Burgundy or something like that, but it was cool nonetheless. I didn't get too many specifics, but Valentino did show me a tattoo that each male member of the family had. That certainly upped his rebel-chicness level . . . and my interest in him. I might have even been growing fond of him.

Against all yearnings of our passionate fury, we did eventually leave his house on Sunday afternoon. Valentino took me to a nearby charming medieval village. We had a lovely time exploring the narrow laneways and touring the ancient castle. It was a truly *Princesse* afternoon and the perfect end to my romantic getaway weekend.

Farewells at the station were coupled with promises to visit each other soon. I didn't really think much would come of our *aventure* besides some good memories—but then again, I really was in search of a summer fling and with a little effort, this time it could actually work out! How long was a summer fling officially supposed to last? I guessed it would ideally be a few weeks of intense passion—but with the distance involved, a few romantic weekends would probably count . . . I'd be ready to tackle finding a more serious relationship at my own speed in autumn once I'd regained my confidence.

Valentino didn't forget about me after my return to Paris. Almost every day, my phone chimed with a new romantic message.

VALENTINO [07/10/05 6:52 PM]

If we must only keep the best to
live life to the fullest, I will keep
every moment we spent together.

How can a girl not fall for a line like that?

VALENTINO [07/11/05 8:43 PM]

How was your day, Canadian Tigresse?
Are your memories still alive or are
they slowly fading away?

Valentino was indeed proving that the French deserve their reputation for being ardent *amoureux*. I wouldn't say I was falling head over heels for Valentino but I'd at least temporarily succumbed to his seductive charm.

VALENTINO [07/12/05 9:52 PM]

If little lily would like me to come to Paris
the weekend of July 29th let me know . . .

Mais bien sûr! Hurrah! It was looking like I would have a successful summer fling after all! July 29th would come quickly enough; nonetheless, I was eagerly counting down the days.

Fourteen. Seven. Two. Wednesday came and went without news. One. Ditto for Thursday. No word. Zilch, zero, *rien*.

He was supposed to come on Friday, but as the day slowly transitioned into evening, I still hadn't heard from him. What had happened to my tireless charmer? Had he been kidnapped by a rival branch of the Calabrian mafia? A message finally came through about 10:00 pm saying he'd had a work emergency and couldn't make it. By then I'd already polished off a few "poor me" glasses of wine—at home, alone—to cushion my disappointment. This was not cool. Why hadn't he let me know before?

His return to the world of messaging was accompanied by fresh promises to try to come the following weekend . . . but come the next weekend, my hopes were once again sadly dashed by a no-show, and I was left in the arms of my *Saint Amour* wine. Nor was he able to come the following weekend. *What had happened to my summer fling?* I'd now wasted a whole precious month waiting around for *Monsieur Invisible!*

It was now August and I was heading off on holiday, alone and romantically empty-handed; my only victory was apparently another notch on my "failed attempt at a summer fling" belt. And of all places, I was going to Italy. Could I find a *real* Italian Romeo there?

"You're really better off without him, Lily," lectured Special Kay.

"Besides, you wouldn't want to keep having to going to . . . Pontiers!" added Pussycat, thick with country disdain.

"It's not *Pontiers*, it's Poitiers!" I corrected her exasperatedly. *How long would this scolding last?*

"And someone with both mafia connections and living

outside Paris . . . now that's a recipe for disaster!" exclaimed Naughty.

"Sigh! You girls might be right," I woefully admitted.

"*Might* . . .?" questioned Naughty, raising an eyebrow.

They had been right from the start. It was near the end of August and we were all back in Paris, belatedly celebrating my birthday at Special Kay's. I didn't completely regret having my *romantique aventure* weekend with Valentino; I just didn't understand why he'd pulled this disappearing act. I hadn't heard from him at all since leaving on holiday—not even for my birthday, which he'd promised to remember. He'd seemed positively 100% into me; maybe not in a "you're my soul mate" way, but, it was supposed to be a **summer** *aventure,* not a single **weekend** one. And with no news from him, the little boost to my ego was quickly dissipating . . . Our male-bashing was interrupted by my ringing phone.

"Hello?"

"Hi Lily; it's Valentino." *Well, well, well,* maybe his memory had finally returned, or his ears might have been ringing loudly enough to compel him to call.

"Oh, hello . . . *Valentino,*" I mustered in my iciest voice. Upon hearing who was on the other end of the line, the girls faces morphed from shock to anxious anticipation, compelling me to flee to Kay's bedroom for some privacy. I wasn't going to let their objections get the better of me. Maybe Valentino had a good reason for not contacting me . . . in weeks!

"Something happened to me the other day," he spurted out after some painful small talk.

"Oh really, what was that?" I prodded.

"I had a surprise visitor last Saturday."

"And who was that?" This was going to be like pulling teeth.

"My ex-girlfriend, and she wasn't alone . . ."

Not alone? Had she come with her own flirtatiously incestuous sibling? I'd had enough with the guessing game.

"Well, go on, tell me; who did she come with, Valentino?" *And why would I care to know?*

"She came to introduce me to . . . my son."

What? Introduce him to his *son?* How insane and downright unbelievable was that? He went on to tell me that his ex-girlfriend, who lived in a remote corner in the northwest of France, and whom he hadn't seen for approximately **nine** months, had just shown up on his doorstep, baby and suitcases in hand, ready to move in. Was this normal French behavior? Supposedly, after they'd broken up, she'd cut off contact and hadn't told him she was pregnant. The story was so absurd that it could only be true. Regardless, I didn't have much of a choice but to accept it. I hadn't tried to contact him in weeks, so it wasn't like he owed me anything or needed to make up some excuse so that I would leave him alone, making his crazy story all the more credible.

Boy, oh, boy—literally! Had I become some kind of weirdo magnet? Could I only pick out the extremely complicated *garçons* of the lot? So far, they'd either been too out of reach for some unfortunate reason or another (Julio + girlfriend; Julien + mountain shepherd boy retreat + too young; now Valentino + ex-girlfriend + baby = triple yikes!), or not far *enough* out of reach (Bobbie, need I say more!). I was beginning to wonder if it was just bad luck or if I wasn't really supposed to have my little summer fling. In any case, my faith in finding one was diminishing, along with the hot summer *je t'aime*-able days. It was almost September and the summer was almost coming to a close. I wasn't quite ready to give up on my quest. If my search was to continue—and finally be successful—I would have to follow some new resolutions.

♥

LIAM [09/05/05 7:20 PM]
Thinking of you . . . hope you're well.

fermé pour congés annuels
(closed.for annual summer holidays)

DAVE [08/25/05 6:36 PM]

Hope you had a lovely holiday.
Can't wait to see you soon at the usual.

Summer Fling Resolutions - August

- Stay away from ~~Spanish/Italian~~ Mediterranean men, especially if they have links with the mafia!

- Avoid any bar pick-ups! They should technically be considered part of the bar boys category (see FIRST resolution list! (And stick to it!)

- Find out immediately where potential candidate lives (answer must be **Paris** . . . but should also be living in non-ghetto districts of the city)

- If he mentions an ex-girlfriend, try to find out the last time he might have slept with said ex (i.e. could she be carrying his child?) (Could I *really* ask this?)

- Don't fall for romantic text messages (no matter *how* romantic!)

- Don't take the train in pursuit of a summer fling! (That's twice in a row now—maybe it's just bad luck with train

DANGEROUS BETS

FROM: MARIO W.   Tuesday, October 4 2005 11:55 PM

Hi, I was wondering what the e-mail address was for Lily
Heise. I'd appreciate you letting me know.
Thanks, Mario W.

Time was standing still . . . perhaps merely for a split
second, but long enough for Cupid's arrow to strike . . .
and hard.

The summer might have been on the brink of ending, but
the *Indian summer* was just beginning! This was always such a
beautiful time in Paris, almost as good as spring! The days
were a little shorter, but it was still sunny and warm—perfect
conditions for love to be lazily aloft!

To make the most of the last days of summer, I'd
organized an early-evening picnic and open-air cinema for the
Canadian group, to coincide with their return from a hike
(one of the other main activities of the club, and one which
I categorically avoided—how could I have fun on Saturday
nights if I had to get up at the crack of dawn the next day to
trudge through the forest? And why would I ever want to
trudge through the forest anyway?).

We, the lazy loafers who hadn't gone on the hike, had arrived at the park beforehand to find a good movie-viewing spot and, of course, to get the picnic started. Paris has many great free events in summer, but one of our favorites was the open-air cinema at the Parc de la Villette. Situated in the northeast of the city (very close to Bobbie's place), the land and buildings used to be the sprawling former wholesale meat market of Paris. The cinema event was far from a modern day "meat market"; however, the friendly atmosphere created by the group picnics could potentially lead to new encounters. I really didn't have any romantic intentions behind arranging the event that night; I was happy to be out and about, needing to get my mind off the disappointment of Valentino—what better way to forget than with some nice *rosé* and good company?

Worn-out hikers began arriving in dribs and drabs, joining our relaxed group of picnic enthusiasts who were now happily sipping chilled wine and nibbling on strong cheese, fresh baguette and other miscellaneous party favors. Among a small group of newly-arrived hikers was someone I'd never seen before: an attractive stranger—accompanied by Cupid and his arrow.

Our eyes locked, and he held me in a deep gaze for what seemed like forever. I think Cupid must have shot arrows at both of us! There have only been a few times when fate has struck me that hard, and I instantly knew that something was going to happen between us. Who was this tall, sexy mystery-man?

Eventually, someone must have interrupted our frozen moment, but there was no undoing Cupid's effect. The newcomer sat down on an empty patch of blanket, his piercing gaze darting towards me every few minutes. We offered him a glass of wine and drilled him with the usual getting-to-know-you questions. It turned out that he'd recently arrived in Paris, having moved down from Amsterdam. He was Dutch-Canadian. *What a great mix*, I thought, and he was oh so very cute. I loved Dutch boys, not only for their tall statures and good looks, but also for their divine sweetness . . . and their accents were to die for. I even had a certain sweetheart in Amsterdam who popped in and out of my life from time to time, though with the distance, we'd never tried seeing each other seriously (in retrospect with my summer of disappearing men, maybe I should have given him a call months ago?). There was something a little strange about this new cute Dutchie, that being his very un-Dutch sounding name: *Mario*. He explained that his parents had wanted to give him an international name—Mario seemed more Italian than anything else, but from my experience, I should just stay away from the name game (and perhaps Italians?). Mario wasn't a typical blond, blue-eyed Dutchman: he had light brown hair and, from what I could gather, green or hazel eyes, but he certainly had Dutch height and he *definitely* had that sexy Dutch allure that made me swoon.

Unfortunately, he didn't stay too long, as the hike had been exhausting (yet *another* reason not to bother partaking in them), and although he left at the same time as a girl who had arrived to the picnic in the same group, it really didn't seem like cupid's arrows had struck the two of them and so my hopes weren't dashed. Mario might have left, but the powerful image of his amazing sparkling eyes continued to effervesce in my mind. Dusk was setting in and soon the movie was going to begin. We packed up our picnic goods, refilled our glasses, and got ready for the night's film: *Dangerous Liaisons* . . .

I couldn't get Mario off my mind. When would I get a chance to see his sparkling irises again? Would I actually have to go on . . . *a hike?* *Ugh*, there had to be another way to see him. As painful as the idea of trekking through the woods (*allll* day) was, I was almost willing to go to such dreadful lengths. To spare myself the agony, I instead put on my investigator's cap. If he'd already gone on a hike, then he was most likely on our mailing list, to which I, as Activities Coordinator, had access. I logged in, typed "Mario" into the search box and hit "Enter". There couldn't be that many Canadian "Marios" in our address book. . .

Voilà! In just a few clicks I had his full name and email address. I was rather proud of my P.I. mission; though, successful as it was, what was I supposed to do with my precious find? I couldn't just drop him a line . . . or, could I? *What would I say?* 'Hey there, hot new member! Have you been properly initiated into the club? Care to meet for a drink?' I would need a really clever excuse to contact him, an ingenious plot of some kind. I couldn't mess up my one last chance at a summer fling—or, what could potentially be even **more** than a summer fling! In fact, I was ready to move on from all this fling-think: it could be nice for a little romance to actually develop.

I had a really good feeling this time around.

I was busily scheming over the perfect plan when the next Canadian Club pub night came up. I'd been avoiding holding them at *The Reindeer* since the Julio incident; I would go back there when I was ready. Who needed Julio, or *The Reindeer*, anyway? This time we were meeting at a new Canadian bar that had recently opened—hopefully there might also be some cute *new* boys joining us. Out with the old and in with the new!

I arrived precisely on time, eagerly scanning the crowd but, alas, no sexy Dutchmen in sight, so I chatted to my friends while keeping a close eye on the door. About an hour into our meet-up, fate came calling . . . with Mr. Mario in tow. I couldn't believe my luck! And this time he'd come accompanied with another guy friend—and not a *girl* like at the post-hike picnic—so perhaps he really was up for grabs?

I agonizingly waited for him to come over and talk to me, which he soon did. My heart immediately sped up. It was exceedingly hard to keep my composure, act smart, and most importantly, not screw things up by saying something stupid. Our successfully light and witty conversation gradually led to our making a very dangerous bet: one that would immensely alter the path of our story.

The basis of the bet itself was a little trivial: Oktoberfest was about to start in Germany and we had gotten to talking about where it was celebrated in Canada. The biggest event is held in a neighboring city to where I went to university, which, not so surprisingly, happens to have a large German population. He claimed it was in a different place, the sister city to where it officially takes place.

"Do you wanna bet on it?" he dared, staring me down with his shining eyes.

"Sure," I said, confident I would win. "What are we betting on?"

"How about a bottle of wine?" he proposed coyly.

"Okay, sounds good." And we sealed the deal with a handshake.

I was ecstatic over having seen him, though in the days that followed the bet, thoughts of Mario had drifted from my mind. I was quite confident that I'd be seeing him sometime soon, at least at another club event. This peaceful state of mind was jolted the following week when I was checking the Club's email account and saw a message from the exact email address for him that I'd tracked down.

FROM: MARIO W.   Tuesday, October 4 2005 11:55 PM

Hi, I was wondering what the e-mail address was for Lily Heise. I'd appreciate you letting me know.
Thanks, Mario W.

My heart stopped dead in its tracks. Could it be true? Was *Mario* actually trying to contact *me*? I somehow calmed myself enough to reply to his message—on behalf of the Club—without giving my identity away. He had no way of knowing that I'd seen his message. I was so excited! I was still proud of my previous detective work . . . but if he would make the first move, that would make me feel even better!

The wait was *paaaiinful*. I must have checked my inbox a trillion times the next day, but it yielded nothing from my dreamy Mario. *Hmmph!* I've never been very skilled in patience, but I knew I had to resist any and all temptation to write to him first. What was taking him so long?

After several extremely torturous days, I *finally* received his reply at my personal account:

FROM: MARIO W.   Thursday, Oct 6 2005 3:37 PM

Hi Lily, Remember me? From the pub night, we talked about the Oktoberfest back home. Now I reckon you are right. So, yes, I will get you a bottle of wine. What color do you wish: white/red/rosé? Where and when can I drop it off?

Well, it was very unmanly, but very admirable to have admitted his defeat. Still, I had trouble believing he didn't have some ulterior, *manly* motives in following through with his end of the bargain. If he'd go out of his way to try to find me, then obviously he liked me, right? If not, why would he be wasting his time?

We played a little email tag during which—solely out of goodwill—I offered to share my prize with him. He appreciatively accepted my gesture and suggested that, since we were still having this Indian summer weather, we could meet after work to make good on the bet somewhere central, perhaps along the Seine. What a great (and indeed *très romantique*) idea—wine *apéro* Parisian sunsets are certainly romantic; maybe Mario was as well?

However, as our bet-repaying date approached, so did dark, brooding clouds. It was certainly not a night for a light picnic on a picturesque bridge overlooking Notre Dame.

"Well, why don't you just come over to my place? I can make us something to eat and we can enjoy the wine here?" was his solution.

Sly . . . It was almost as if he'd ordered up those menacing clouds to force us indoors. I should really have known that it was awfully dangerous to go over to someone's place just like that (remember Spanish Bobbie's dinner tactics?). But since it was my heart leading, not my head, I agreed to his backup plan, thereby setting in motion the wheels of fate—or maybe they'd already started back at the picnic and I was merely their helpless cog.

Mario lived neared Place de la Nation, a rather calm, residential area in eastern Paris, near the edge of the city bordering the large Bois de Vincennes park which gave the neighborhood an added plus for the outdoorsy type. It was therefore not surprising that Mario lived around here. Exiting the *métro*, I imagined him going for runs in the vast park, all hot and sweaty. Reaching the top of the steps, my divine dream became the real thing (well, minus the sweat): Mario, eyes sparkling, gentlemanly escorted me down the few streets back to his nice, loft-style apartment.

After a quick tour of the place, he gave me the choice of one of two wines for my prize: a Californian or a French one. I let the French wine snob in me be challenged by the Californian. Not fretting too much over what to feed a vegetarian (in meat-centric France, I was used to being served a simple salad or a pile of plain steamed vegetables), Mario easily came up with some delicious veggie-friendly pasta (maybe he was actually a little Italian?). Our chatty conversation flowed just as easily as the wine and, before we knew it, we'd finished our meal, the French bottle was being uncorked and we were settling down on the sofa.

Did I mention that Mario was really cute? And tall? Plus, I liked his international allure; Mario had gone full circle: his Dutch parents had raised him in Montreal and now, here he was, back in Europe. While he was more business-like than

I usually preferred, he was funny, interesting and, up to that point, very nice. I also felt that there was a special connection between us.

With our wine bottle empty, Mario offered me some cognac—*pourquoi pas?* The night was going quite well, so why stop there? Another silly bet was made, which I was sure to lose, but that was just a great excuse for us to see each other again soon. I was certain that Mario would be the final candidate to wrap up the quest; I couldn't have been happier!

The amazing cloud of bliss I was floating on was about to run into those nasty menacing clouds in the real-world sky. Mario brutally brought me back down to earth. He was about to be sent to Africa for work. My heart sank. *Africa . . . ?* Why does everyone have to go away? And why so very **far** away? Why couldn't it be somewhere relatively nearby, like London, or Brussels, or even Poitiers? I tried not to let the news bother me too much; maybe he'd be coming back every once in a while? And it didn't sound like the transfer was 100% confirmed anyway; could there still be hope?

In my state of dismay and mid-level drunkenness, I was caught off guard by Mario's intensified gaze (he may have even slid a little closer to me on the sofa).

"We have the same eye color," he declared with strict seriousness.

"Oh really, is that so?" was probably all I could fumble out.

Before I knew it, I was being yanked off the sofa, apparently to verify this earth-shattering discovery in the mirror. There we were staring into each other's eyes—into our own green-eyed likeness. I think it was too much for him and he cracked, suddenly swirling me around to kiss me (maybe to see if our lips were the same as well?).

We stumbled, still lip-locked, back to the sofa. Lost in passionate euphoria, I barely listened to the suspicious comments he slid in when taking a quick gulp of air.

"I'm not looking for anything serious . . . I'm going to Africa . . . " It was going on 12:30 am and any hope of my catching the last *métro* was fading as quickly as a Dutch sunset.

Ahhhh! What was I supposed to do? I was broken-hearted to learn that he was probably leaving, but my blind optimism didn't want to believe that—hadn't fate flung us together? *Something* had to be meant to be, whatever it was. Even if nothing happened, I **really** wanted him, and even if he was actually going to be leaving in a few months, something (here and now) was better than nothing at all (or so my alcohol-infused rationale was telling me). I was a modern woman, liberated; I should embrace these sorts of experiences.

But there would always be consequences . . .

And so I stayed. Mario certainly didn't disappoint on the passion scale. But I was soon sleeplessly tossing and turning in an unknown and uncomfortable bed, hypothesizing on what would happen next.

Mario was pretty sweet to me the following day; since we were both heading for work in the same direction, we took the *métro* together from the peaceful woods of Vincennes across the city to *La Défense*, the business district to the west of Paris, and its forest of impersonal skyscrapers. When we parted ways, he gave me a long tender kiss good-bye amidst the rush of scurrying suit-clad Parisian office workers.

With this, I decided that things were looking on the positive side for a Dutch lover, albeit a (possibly) temporary one. I thought that, even if he would be leaving soon, maybe we could see each other a little before he left, and this could fulfill my quest for a pick-me-up fling . . . even though I was now wanting more.

I returned to my plot-scheming to figure out how to see Mario again as soon as possible. Seeing as I'd lost our second bet, I had a good excuse to contact him—to give him his duly-earned prize of a bottle of wine. So, I invited him over for dinner and planned an impressive gourmet spread to accompany his liquid reward.

At the time—the end of October—I was getting ready to finally move from my itsy bitsy, *miniscule* bachelor pad into a bigger one-bedroom place just around the corner, which happened to be also owned by my quirky old landlady. Though I would miss the gorgeous view of the city, I certainly wouldn't miss the six flights of stairs, nor the boisterous *Chez François* bar across the street. When I mentioned to Mario that I was moving the following week, he graciously offered to help me carry some boxes to my new place before dinner. It might have been fun to have a little snog there in the empty new apartment, but we behaved ourselves, simply dropping off some things before heading back to my old place to eat. It would be my last dinner there; and, it would be one I would probably never forget.

Everything was going rather nicely. We'd enjoyed Mario's prize wine and were sipping a crisp *digestif* over dessert when he started to get a little weird, even antsy.

"I have to tell you something." *Oh mon dieu!* That line almost always paves the way for bad news.

"Okay, what . . .?" I hesitantly asked, hoping the news wouldn't hinder my progress on finally having my belated summer fling.

"I actually have a girlfriend."

I could tell that he'd been trying to muster up enough courage to say something, but this was the last thing I'd expected him to cough up! I guessed he also had amnesia, because he certainly hadn't acted like he had a girlfriend the last time I'd seen him. But instead of throwing the rest of my cognac in his face (what a waste—poor cognac!) or slapping him and telling him to go to hell (like he rightfully deserved), I actually took up the anonymous girlfriend's defense. Had he ever thought about her feelings? The consequences of his actions? I doubted Mario ever thought about anything, really; his brain apparently had no control over his body.

After a serious scolding about how he shouldn't be fooling around on his girlfriend, he assured me he didn't want to hurt her and *blah, blah, blah*. Well, he should have thought about that before making dangerous bets he couldn't handle.

What a coward! I could see right through him (well, *now*). By going away to Africa, he wouldn't have to break up with his girlfriend; what this did to him, though, was make him think he had taken a hiatus from the relationship.

I sent him away, slamming the door; somehow I managed to abstain from any name-calling or pushing him down my deadly staircase. I served myself another big glass of cognac, and while I was trying to clean up without breaking the dishes he had used, I got a lame text message from him saying something like he wasn't an angel and that nobody was perfect—again, *blah, blah, blah!* I promptly deleted it, downed my cognac and poured myself another one.

I couldn't believe it. How could I have been such a fool? Why had fate been such an evil trickster? I'd been disappointed about the failure of the other summer fling candidates, but none of them had affected me this badly. Maybe that was just it: I hadn't taken the others very seriously, whereas I'd allowed myself to think that something more could happen with Mario. This time it wasn't a bruised ego I was left with; it was a wounded *je ne t'aime pas* heart. I wasn't sure what it would take to mend it. I was beginning to wonder if I should I just give up searching for a little fling all together. However, I wasn't sure if I was really ready to accept defeat.

❤️

HANS [10/27/05 10:57 PM]
Tigresse! I miss you darling!

DAVE [10/28/06 6:28 PM]
I haven't seen you in ages,
free for a drink?

"I might have to agree. He probably should have been honest with you from the start but, in all fairness, polygamy is an acceptable practice in many cultures."

"I don't care if it's an acceptable custom elsewhere; it certainly isn't okay in my books! And besides, Mario isn't from a country where it *is* allowed."

"That's true; however, it's hard to find everything you are looking for in just *one* person. I don't see anything wrong with dating two complimentary women. In fact, I think that would be the ideal situation."

"Dave! You're coming up with the perfect excuse for all the cheating men out there!" I screeched, getting a little fed up with all this adulterous talk; it was still too fresh after the Mario upset. "What about loving someone just as they are?"

"I've actually come to the conclusion that I'll never find everything I'm looking for in just one person . . . well, except in just this one girl in particular . . ." I got what he was hinting at and decided it was about time to leave, urgently waving at the waiter.

"Poor Mario," Dave continued, "he fell under your charm and forgot about his girlfriend . . . or should I say, lucky Mario? Will I ever be that lucky . . .?"

"*L'addition!*" I yelped at the waiter. "*Maintenant!*"

(Indian) Summer Fling Resolutions - October

- Stay away from Mediterranean men or **FAKE** Mediterranean men

    - or REAL Dutchmen

    - or green-eyed cuties

    - or hikers (?)

    - or CUPID'S ARROW!

- Learn from mistakes: even if a guy is flirting with you, he could still have a girlfriend, try to find this out **immediately**

- Ask leading questions to see if candidate has any plans to leave country

- Ask other memory questions to see if any amnesiac tendencies are evident

- Don't be blinded by seemingly fateful signs (see May resolutions)

- Dating equation: "I'm not looking for anything serious" = I really am not looking for anything serious <u>or</u> I actually have a girlfriend

- Don't make bets—ever again!

IRISH TRICK OR TREAT

[bar boys don't send texts]

Were there two men in my apartment? One in my bed, the other . . .

November 1st is a public holiday in Catholic countries. It's the day you are supposed to pay respect to your beloved deceased, as well as visit their graves. It also just happens to fall perfectly on the day after Halloween, allowing revelers to recover in peace. It's rather strange that Anglo-Saxon countries have never added this holiday to their calendars. The French really aren't that religious, except when it comes to their public holidays. I was all for this expression of faith: *vive les vacances!*

Special Kay and I always liked to do something on Halloween, even if it wasn't much celebrated in France. In fact, celebrating it here was a fairly recent fad; so, the French approach to Halloween was limited to cobwebs or mini pumpkins displayed in storefront windows. Even the few who dressed up for parties were almost exclusively disguised as witches, regardless of their gender. We'd discovered this fact on our first Halloween out in Paris, the night we ended up at *La Piñata* salsa bar (where I'd met Bobbie), with the oddly-costumed Chilean male witch. In Paris, you won't find anyone dressed as Darth Vadar, Wonder Woman or a bumblebee (North American costumes, to be sure). I usually tried to find a compromise: keep a macabre theme, but one with a twist (my favorite costume I'd come up with was probably a racy 'devil in a blue dress' for my first Halloween in Paris). This year it would be just Kay and I going out. We hadn't planned on dressing up, but I put on a Gothic-inspired black dress and, with the help of a few cheap plastic spiders and old fishnet stockings adorning my arms, I had become a 'Spider Lady' and was ready to climb into the night of the dead.

I was happy not to be all alone that particular night, as it was my last chance to invite someone over to my room with a view; I would officially begin living in my new apartment as of the next day: November 1st. Some good wine and chatter with Kay would help erase the bad memories of my recent dinner here with a certain devil-in-disguise Dutchman. It would surely also ease me onto the road of recovery; I couldn't let him keep me down for long.

Around midnight, with our jovial spirits alight, we ambled down the hill to one of our Irish Pub hangouts: *O'Hooligan's*. More of a club than a pub, *O'Hooligan's* attracted a good international crowd; however, amidst the guests were some unsavory characters who came because of the low cover charge and the cute foreign girls. Even though we would inevitably have to fend off a few sleazy guys, we usually had fun. Plus on this particular night, it was appropriate to go out to an Irish bar where we were certain to find a festive

Halloween atmosphere . . . and some sexy ghosts or ghouls.

We were having a reasonably good time dancing and adding percentage points to our already substantial blood alcohol content (with some spooky cocktails). During a lull in the music, we sat down to give our feet a rest, and do some people watching. Whether it was the alcohol wearing off, or the crowd lacking tasty eye-candy, Kay must have had some reason for announcing that she had an idea, or rather, a mission.

"Alright, here's the plan. We have to go find someone, kiss him and meet back here in five minutes."

"Okay!" I agreed enthusiastically. We'd never done anything quite like this before (and it was highly unusual behavior for the normally reserved Special Kay). If the men wouldn't come to us, we would just go to them! This was a novel way to add some spice to our night . . . so off we went.

I took the mission very seriously and in about one minute I'd found my target: a tallish, broad-shouldered, sandy blond good-looking chap. I assessed the situation for another 20 seconds; he seemed to be with just a male friend, and no girlfriend in sight. He would do. I launched my attack mission, code name: "Kiss and Run"—which is pretty much what I did. I went up to him, grabbed his collar and spontaneously kissed him on the lips, disappearing as quickly as I'd appeared. I must have been back at our table in less than three minutes.

Confident and proud of the follow-through of my mission, I sat back and waited for Kay. What seemed like an eternity (probably about eight minutes) went by before I went to track her down. There she was, actually *talking* to her victim, and he didn't seem to want to free her up. The D.J.

started playing tunes we approved of, so I dragged her onto the dance floor in an attempt to get rid of her new friend and pursue our evening of adventure. Her suitor followed. She soon realized that she had chosen the wrong target and spent the better part of the night trying to ditch him.

I'd almost forgotten about my victim when he appeared by my side.

"Hi there," he shyly started.

"Oh! Hi . . . *umm* . . . you."

"Chris." He introduced himself. Chris was Irish, and he was cute, even when I subtracted the fact of his adorable accent. We got to talking, and being the noble woman I am, I decided to admit our little mission. Luckily, he didn't seem to mind being the target of our fun. After all, how often do random attractive strangers come up and kiss you without any prior warning? We carried on talking and dancing and, soon enough, I had another cocktail in hand. I believe that turned into several more, because before I knew it I was awoken by a knock on my door. Looking around, I realized that I was in the virtually-empty bedroom of my new apartment . . . and apparently I wasn't alone!

From what my sleepy, hung-over mind could gather, there were two men present: one who'd just entered the living room, and the other cuddled up next to me on a thin mattress on the floor (IKEA was great for cheap design, but certainly didn't win points for timely delivery).

Who was at the door? My brain was slowly sobering. *Ugh!* I'd forgotten my landlady's handyman was scheduled to come by to do some fix-up work to my new place, and that he had a key! The bedroom door was wide open and I didn't have enough time to jump up to close it, so I snapped my eyes shut, pretending to be asleep. Luckily, upon seeing us, he discreetly left. Damn . . . that would have to be dealt with later. Even though it was a slightly awkward situation, I was actually sort of relieved. The handyman was a nice enough guy in his mid-30s, but last year he'd started calling me up to see if I was free for coffee, which I never was. At least now he would think I had a boyfriend (whether it was true or not) and leave me alone.

Back to the first problem . . . who was in my bed?

It seemed that I hadn't done too poorly with my trick-or-treating, bringing home a loot bag filled with one Irish cutie. Memories of the end of the night were rather foggy; it was Halloween after all, a night of surprises . . . but had I come home with a trick or a treat? Could it be that I'd finally found the right candidate (or in this case: candy-date) for my little fling?

After he left, I gave these recent events some serious thinking. He did seem like a good match: nice, good-looking, and apparently not too clingy; however, there was just one catch . . . had I given him my phone number? I scrolled through my phone contacts and, alas, didn't see any new or unlabeled numbers.

I was a complete failure at this summer fling business. *Hopeless!* The sun and the amorous energy of Paris were gradually being overtaken by endless grey skies, whose chilly drizzle was washing away any hope of finding some warm summer loving. It was November and I now really had no other choice but to retreat, and go into a deep romantic hibernation. A break would do me good; it would give me time to reflect on my quest and see if it was even worth pursuing next spring.

I would have to do something: either improve my strategies, or replace my mission all together. However, would the *je t'aime* vibes of Paris cooperate?

VALENTINO [11/06/05 8:35 PM]
Hello Lily just a little message to say that you
are always welcome in my home and in my heart

fermé jusqu'au 3 janvier – Bonnes Fêtes!
(closed until January 3rd – Happy Holidays!)

DAVE [12/25/05 7:55 PM]

Wishing you a very Merry Christmas,
next year is bound to bring you
everything you desire!

General New Year's Resolutions - 2006

- Stay in hibernation until **SPRINGTIME**. Then:
- Stay away from Mediterraneans, or "fake" Mediterranean men (wouldn't hurt to add Irish men to this list; but it was probably my fault Chris didn't have my number to call . . .)
- Check I.D. (which will handle both the age and the Mediterranean issue)
- Try to suss out anyone who might be capable of pulling a disappearing act . . . or hiding a girlfriend . . . or any children (or both!)
- Avoid any and every invitation for dinner at his place on first date
- Do your best to stay away from any foreign-themed bars (i.e. Canadian, South American, Irish)
- Random spontaneous kissing might not be the best tactic to finding a fling
- No more trick-or-treating! (I know Halloween is ten months away . . . but still)
- Don't give out phone number – but don't forget to **get** phone numbers

AND MOST IMPORTANTLY, REDEFINE YOUR QUEST:

OUT WITH THE SUMMER FLING—IN WITH THE

"SUMMER ROMANCE"

<u>BAD</u> BLAIR AND THE BORDELA

BLAIR [03/20/06 3:47 PM]
Bordela cocktails are deadly,
aren't they?

"How did it get to be so late?"

"More like how did it get to be so *early?* Mom is totally going to kill us!"

It was spring, and after several months of romantic slumber, I was officially waking from hibernation—but to what? Gone would be the negative boys of last year. I vowed to not make the same mistakes, learn my lessons, and follow my New Year's resolutions. To ensure my success this year, I decided to modify my quest: I would not be seeking out a "summer fling." Instead, I would be searching for what I deemed to be a *romance d'été*. My heart had somewhat healed during the winter's hiatus, but my overall confidence still needed a boost. I wanted more than a fling, but I still didn't think I needed to find the man of my dreams either.

Yes, a new and fresh start it would be! There had to be the perfect "summer romance" candidate out there, and who better to get the new season kicked off with than one of the greatest adventurers I know: my dear sister. *Très belle* and loads of fun, Cori was always the source of entertaining exploits, had incredible stamina, was usually the last standing at parties . . . and she was coming to Paris! However, my sister wasn't visiting alone; she was coming with our mother, who on this particular evening/morning was undoubtedly **not** sound asleep back at my place, certainly worrying about the lives of her precious daughters, out loose in the City of Light (a term which could mean many things . . . red light, disco light, morning light . . .).

My sister had visited me before (a trip involving its own set of late-night shenanigans . . . taking us from Paris to Amsterdam), but this was Mom's first time; therefore, we wanted to make it memorable (and we did not disappoint on that level—we would never live this one down!). I'd organized an extra-special trip for us, including travel to the South of France, and Italy for them to meet my surrogate Italian family (whom I'd lived with during my exchange back in high school).

May the adventure begin!

Ma famille arrived on a Friday. Seeing as it was their first day, we just relaxed in my neighborhood, allowing them to get over their jet lag. But the next day was a Saturday—our *only* Saturday night in Paris—and so, we really had to go out on the town (at least the young *filles* anyway).

We started the night off with a relatively tame dinner party at my place along with a few of the girls, so that Mom could take part in some of the festivities and meet my local partners in crime whom she'd heard so much about. Special Kay and Naughty came early, bearing gifts of wine and enthusiastic smiles; Pussycat would join us later. Mom had also brought me a couple of cute presents for such an occasion, including some racy cocktail napkins with the slogan: *Drink till he's cute!* on them. Little did she know, I would take this message literally!

Dinner was complemented by a vast array of wines, which were followed by a few fun shots for good measure before we tucked Mom into bed and crept out into the Saturday night fever of Paris. Before leaving, we promised to be *good* and make it an *early* night. The plan was to go to the *Bordela Braziliana*, a lively bar near Place de la République, the large square just above the Marais district honoring "the French Republic" born from the many revolutions (could the venue start a little revolution in my love life?).

The *Bordela* was a cool yet slightly grungy place; its packed dance floor usually sprawled into the dining area and onto its tabletops. Even though the place exuded lively Brazilian chaos, it surprisingly closed at 3:00 am, fairly "early" for Parisian clubs, and—I would image—*extremely* early compared to real Brazilian *festas*. We thought that going here would force us to go home at a decent hour (well, that was the plan at least when we left my place around 11:30 pm).

Since we arrived relatively early at the *Bordela*, we didn't have to wait long to get in. Yet, once inside, we realized that this short wait meant that this place was kind of slow, and we found the dance floor completely empty. Its sorry state, and the bad music pumping out of the speakers, drove Cori and me straight to the bar. *Dois Mojitos por favor.* Refreshing as they were, they didn't appease us for long, and in no time our straws had sucked up the last of the sugary rum, leaving us to wrestle with our boredom.

"How about a shot?" Cori energetically suggested. *Por que não?* It wasn't much of a Parisian habit to do shots, but as we'd gotten started with some good ones back home, I figured we might as well keep up the momentum. Arriving back at the bar, the bartender seemed incapable of making anything delicious, his only proposal being straight vodka shots. Didn't they have fun shots in Brazil? What did they drink during carnival? Cori and I looked at each other, then at the still-empty dance floor and begrudgingly agreed to the bartender's mediocre offerings. This over-indulgence in the deadly clear stuff would end up being a bad idea . . .

The *Bordela* finally started picking up. Scanning the crowd of newcomers, I caught sight of one of my old flames, a true *Bordela* barfly: Blair, the British bad-boy. *Grrhhh* . . . he wasn't exactly on my "men I want to run into" list; instead he belonged on the "loser/reject boys I'd met in Paris" ranking. Blair and I had something of a 'here, there and nowhere' history. Come to think of it, this night paralleled a similar one, precisely four years prior, when I'd first met Blair. Ever since, he'd popped sporadically in and out of my life—that was, until this fateful *Bordela* outing, which would put a solid end to all that . . . and I wouldn't be the one to come out on the losing end this time.

Back when I was a student in Paris, we used to go to a tiny Dutch bar, the *Pont d'Amsterdam* (maybe this was where my soft spot for the Dutch originated?). Every Monday was international student night, the cheap drinks and fun vibes generally leading to dancing on the tables and a certain amount of miscellaneous trouble with other international party-goers (and the sexy Dutch bartenders . . .). When I'd come back to live in Paris permanently two years later, the *Pont* was less the kind of place I frequented, but now and then it was still good for some nostalgic fun.

On that particular night, I had another foreign visitor staying with me: an Italian friend named Veronica. I decided to take her out to the *Pont* to start off an exciting Saturday night in Paris. On the crowded dance floor, I found myself grooving back-to-back with a tall, cute fellow reveler. Actually, I was only guessing at his cuteness; he *was* behind me after all, but I'd stolen enough quick glances to be intrigued. We gradually started dancing closer, purposefully brushing up against each other until he finally turned around and struck up a conversation. This led to a pint . . . or two . . . or three, and soon enough it was 2:00 am and time for *Le Pont* to close. Not ready to end our night, my new British friend, Blair, invited me, along with his own visiting friend and mine, back to his place for a few (more) drinks. Poor Veronica wasn't the slightest bit interested in his friend, but did me the favor of tolerating conversation with him while Blair was fixing to make out with me. The 'night' ended early the next morning, with Veronica and I creeping onto the *métro* after dawn to catch some winks before taking on Paris in the daylight (*Jeez*, do we see a "bad host" pattern forming here? Was I about to repeat this history with my sister?).

Our initial meeting was way before Stéphane and my "searching for a summer fling" days—at this point in time, I was just looking for a cute boy to hang out with . . . nothing too serious, but not in the fling category either (perhaps an early incarnation of my quest for a summer romance!). I was rather taken by Blair. I loved his posh British accent and, in the light of day, he was indeed rather attractive, with medium blond, wavy hair and a sort of young-Mick-Jagger swagger (and just as cocky!). Blair and I were very similar, leading to our mutual attraction. We were both fun-loving Leos, both smart and sophisticated; however, I was much more mature and drank far less. Blair not only looked like Mick Jagger, he seemed to aspire to be like him in many other ways as well, what with his excess partying and *laisser-faire* attitude.

Blair was also the undeserving holder of a killer job at U.N.E.S.C.O., a position he had landed by pure luck. Working for the U.N. was, by all accounts, a *dream* job— no taxes, interesting projects, a pledge to help save the world, cool international people (Okay, maybe they weren't all cool; I suppose you also had to deal with a few jerks scattered amongst them . . . ones not unlike this particular Brit!). Blair showed up for work whenever he wanted (i.e. 10:00 am, 11:00 am, 12:00 pm . . . or not at all!) and his boss was such a push-over that Blair would never get fired and would only ever leave the job if one day he got too bored (is my mild jealousy apparent?).

Blair and I saw each other a few times just after our *Pont d'Amsterdam* meeting; then he suddenly disappeared into thin air. I was rather miffed by his lack of contact, but after a few unanswered text messages I was *not* going to try again. Unfortunately, this became his trademark. When he got bored he would give me a call, and as it would often coincide with a romantic lull in my life, I would fall for his antics once again. But he would inevitably vanish after a few dates, like he was going off on tour or something.

Years had gone by without us seeing each other and then I ran into him at the *Bordela* a few months before my night out with Cori (okay, I have to admit, I hadn't quite hibernated 100% over the winter . . . maybe just 80%). I was out with the girls and right when a good-looking (but a tad short and probably too young) German guy started chatting me up, tall, suave Blair appeared, his head towering over the other dancers. He came sauntering over and, after I had scolded him for not calling me in ages, he bought me a drink, peace was made, and the poor German guy was left defeated (those Brits can hold their own against the Germans!).

Blair was extra charming this particular time around. He took me out for dinner a few times, texted occasionally, and it even seemed like he had miraculously changed . . . could he have really changed his tune? Alas, he hadn't—and obviously I hadn't learnt my lesson either (same old song and dance from both of us!). And, not a big surprise in retrospect, he soon pulled his usual disappearing act . . . he had no idea it would be his last chance to play on my stage.

So when I spotted him at the *Bordela* on the night out with Cori and the girls, I was understandably rather fed up with him and tried to give him the cold shoulder. As he was coming over to deliver a repetitive chorus line of, "Long time no see! How are things?" I whispered to Cori that it was the infamous Blair. After introductions had been made, they started chatting a bit. She was actually being *nice* to him!

"What are you doing? Don't be so friendly to him!" I seethed through my teeth.

"Why not?" she asked, innocently.

"He hasn't called me in months, that's why!" Apparently

she had confused him with a different ex-ex-ex-boyfriend who lived in London (a.k.a. the recipient of my horrible, accidental Valentine's break-up letter).

Blair was with his adorable new *protégé*: Max. This youthful specimen was a young intern at U.N.E.S.C.O. whom Blair was training to follow in his slimy seductive footsteps.

"You know Blair, Max is so sweet; I hope you're not poisoning him with your evil ways!" I hissed, yanking Cori away to dance.

It was about then that Pussycat showed up with a rich visiting friend (visitors all around!) who offered us another round of those terrible vodka shots. I'm not really sure how many more rounds came after that, but eventually I ended up dancing extremely closely with a tall male . . . and it wasn't Blair . . .

"Lily! Stop falling asleep!" shouted Cori from across the room.

I lifted my head slightly and peered out my left eye. *OMG, where the heck were we?* This didn't look like the *Bordela* at all . . . Slowly pondering this question I posed to myself, I realized a better one would be: *whose lap is my head was propped on?* I dared to open my eyes again and looked up into what seemed to be the heavenly eyes of . . . Keanu Reeves!

How did we get all the way to Hollywood?

No, there was no way we were in California; a quick glance around the room proved we were definitely in some unknown, very Parisian apartment. Relieved that we hadn't been kidnapped into an international ring of human trafficking, I focused on the face belonging to the lap . . .

hmmmm, not a bad catch at all. I mustered just enough energy to sit up, give my catch a kiss on the cheek and prop my head on his shoulder. How many of those vodka shots had I downed? I really shouldn't drink so much when I'm exhausted (exhaustion is always a good excuse for misbehaving and impromptu passing out—kind of like last summer when I met Julien, the shepherd boy). Still, at least my pillow was a dreamy hunk.

Somewhere between the last remembered vodka and our having to leave the closing *Bordela,* I'd managed to pick up this cute half-Asian guy and, since I couldn't remember his name, he became *Keanu.* Cori had thought Keanu was taking us to another club. Unfortunately, this particular club turned out to be *Le Salon*—the living room of the apartment he shared with his sister.

Due to my sporadic passing out, Keanu was trying to keep Cori company and he'd brought out an utterly random selection of alcohol to keep her entertained—maybe not such a good idea after all that wine, the shots back at home, the mojitos . . . and, oh yes, the vodka.

"Hey Lily, wake up!" Out of boredom or a lack of anything good to drink, Cori had begun prodding me to leave. Maybe that wasn't such a bad idea. Keanu called us a cab and out we stumbled into the Paris . . . morning.

"How did it get to be so late?" I questioned, the actual time only dawning on me once outside. Cori and I were totally in for it.

Arriving close to home, we realized we'd spent all of our money on those dreadful shots and I had to leave Cori in the taxi as collateral while I crept inside my place for more cash, and was subjected to a meteor shower of questions and scolding from our sleepy mom. Poor Cori suffered badly for our escapades and lay bedridden the whole next day in complete hangover agony from all the miscellaneous drinks she'd had. Luckily, my Keanu catnap had saved me from a similar fate.

I didn't get a message from cute Keanu the next day, or for that matter, *ever*, as in my state I hadn't bothered to give him my number (*again*—seriously!). Instead I got this one:

BLAIR [03/20/06 3:47 PM]

**Bordela cocktails are deadly,
aren't they?**

I don't think I'd ever gotten a message from Blair within 24 hours of seeing him.

Finally he seemed to care! And he was certainly insanely jealous that he'd lost out. But was it too late . . . ? Had I finally won my freedom from Bad Blair? Hopefully there would be no encore for this particular show.

Boy oh boy, had I ever gotten my summer romance-hunting off to a bad start! Digging up guys from the past was definitely **not** a productive way to achieve any good *je t'aime*-ing. I needed a new *homme*, but I'd clearly missed my chance with the hot Keanu . . . would I nab another?

Back to my resolutions . . .

BLAIR #2 [03/30/06 9:32 PM]

**Hi! Tigresse! I'm Blair from last night in
O'Hooligans! How are you since the
crazy dance we had? Would you
like to have a drink tonight?**

DAVE [04/02/06 16:44 PM]
I miss you. Any chance
you're free tonight?

"It's not really far to give *all* Brits a bad name just from this one bad apple. There are plenty of good ones out there."

"Is that so?"

"Well, you're looking at one," said Dave, with a smile. "They've been known to be quite sweet and tender. Really good catches . . ."

"I'm not so sure about that . . ."

"Okay, well, in popular culture, we're not known to be the best lovers, but that's not really true. We can be extremely faithful and dedicated."

"From my experience, Brits tend to be rather non-committal and quite good at pulling disappearing acts!"

"How anyone could disappear on you is beyond me," he said, his hand creeping across the table.

"I should just stay away from them anyway," I exclaimed with an exaggerated double-handed gesture, in an attempt to get them out of his reach.

"There are many benefits to dating someone who speaks the same language; you are more on the same wave-length, have similar cultural references, can express your feelings better . . ."

"You might have a point there. However, I can't seem to find any right here in Paris."

"Maybe one is right under your nose and you just can't see him . . . did I tell you how pretty you look tonight?" And with that he boldly brushed a stray lock of hair away from my face, out of my vision.

Yikes! Time to go! Should I have added *Avoid going out to the Rendez-vous* as part of my resolutions?

Summer Romance Resolutions - April

- Re-read General Resolutions . . . and stick to them! Especially:

- do your best to stay away from any foreign-themed bars (safe to add Brazilian to previous list)

- Possibly add Brits to the list of nationalities to avoid (and definitely avoid ANYONE called Blair)

- Okay, it's good I remembered not to openly give out phone number—but I need to at least **get** phone numbers (must have forgotten this one during my hibernation)

- Along a similar vein – get at least first name as well

- Stay away from ex-fling candidates: once flung, should be flung for good

- Stay away from anyone too suave/cool—nothing but trouble!

- Don't give a guy a **tenth** try—he certainly won't have changed!

- Avoid vodka shots ... *clearly* dangerous!

- Throw out the "Drink till he's cute!" napkins!

    AND: Stay away from the Rendez-vous!

COME FLY WITH ME . . .

FROM: DEAN   Monday, 1 May 2006 5:09 PM

You seem like the type of gal that enjoys adventures too . . .

It was the start of spring, the absolute best time to do the casting for my summer romance. I had to get it right this year. However, it looked like I really needed to actually follow my resolutions. Dave was absolutely correct. I couldn't banish anyone because of his nationality. However, as much as I wanted something fun, I had so much trouble with fiery Latinos, or just plain over-romantic types, that I might want to avoid them. Blair was certainly a bad example of a Brit, yet thinking about it, maybe it could make sense to leave the romantic door open for an Anglophone; at least we would have enough similar cultural references, and we should be able to communicate clearly together (in theory!). There were plenty of other English-speaking men in Paris! Why not try an American, or a *real* Canadian (Mario didn't really count)? Surely I could find some good ones (or just *one*) here in Paris? Paris was full of young Hemingways, transferred businessmen (preferably International Men of Mystery or I.M.M. for short), and various embassy (or U.N. / U.N.E.S.C.O.—*grrrbh!*) staffers. Yet, the problem wasn't the quantity, but the quality. Actually, an I.M.M. would be perfect. James Bond-esque! I wouldn't be too picky; I would easily settle on the Pierce Brosnan or Daniel Craig model. Where should I go looking for a potential I.M.M., expat lover? Or rather, how could I put myself in a position for one to find **me**? I was an ocean away from the best of them . . . *or was I?*

—Last call for Flight 69 to Montreal, boarding at Gate 20—

I hastily grabbed another bottle of champagne from the duty-free shop and zoomed over to my departure gate.

My dear friend *Princesse J.* was getting married and I just had to attend the royal wedding. Hailing from the same kingdom (or rather, colony), *Princesse J.* and I had met years ago while working together at my first job in France. With none of the French frogs she'd kissed turning into *Prince Charmant, Princesse J.* returned to our distant native land, where she joyfully found herself the perfect prince. Now her fairytale was coming to a close with the perfect happy-ending wedding, an occasion I absolutely could not miss. Bags packed with some special celebratory bubbly and an essential cute red dress to wear on the big day, off I went, dragging my bottle-rattling suitcase to the airport behind me.

When taking planes, especially early in the morning, most travelers wear comfortable clothes. I, however, was still in my "must look cute on all occasions" mode—you never know when you could run into a sexy romantic contender. So here I was, in a pretty, though rather inappropriate-for-sitting-boxed-into-a-tiny-airplane-seat-for-eight-hours outfit (short-ish skirt, figure-fitting sweater-set combo, and even heels), boarding my west-bound plane. I strutted down the aisle towards A22. As I scanned ahead, trying to spot my designated seat, my eyes met the gaze of another passenger sitting about halfway down the row, whose eyes remained glued to me as I gradually made my way closer. I could almost read his thoughts: "I sure wish that *belle fille* was sitting next to me." *Your wish is my command!* This was part of the *Princesse* fairytale after all.

"Excuse me, I believe that's my seat," I announced, pointing to the empty one next to him. It seemed to be his lucky day . . . and maybe mine as well?

This wasn't the first time I'd been seated next to a potential romantic interest on a flight. The previous year, on a Vancouver-bound plane to visit my mother in Victoria, British Columbia (she'd abandoned the small town where I'd grown up, soon after I had), I was seated next to a suave French wine exporter off to sell his delicious wares to the West. *Ohhh! A wine exporter!* I was totally thrilled . . . at first.

He kept me entertained with lively banter and extra mini bottles of wine he'd managed to charm from the flight attendants. However, over the course of our chatting, I'd managed to completely bewitch him and, as we neared Vancouver, he got a little weird, declaring that he was going to skip out on his client appointments and come to Victoria with me. As much as this sounded like a tantalizing proposition, there was no way I was taking this guy with me. My mom would have killed me (this was before her trip to Paris)! She was expecting some French specialties, but not in the flesh and blood. He was also getting a little too clingy (as I've said before, the French can fall easily IN love but just as easily fall OUT of it). Disembarking from the flight, I took his business card, said I'd be in touch and raced off to collect my luggage and escape to my next flight before he got a chance to buy a plane ticket to tail me.

However, this time around, I got a totally different vibe from my co-passenger. He quickly struck up a conversation, which would last most of the flight. His name was Dean and he was from the U.S., but was working in Canada, hence his presence on this flight. But what had brought him to France?

"So, Dean, what were you doing in Europe?" I curiously inquired.

"I was in Brussels for work." *Hmmm* . . . intriguing: traveling for work. That upped his chances of being an I.M.M. He probably traveled a lot, coming and going between North America and Europe. That was an exciting profile for a passionate summer romance applicant.

"Oh, really? Doing some work with a European institution?" I pressed on.

"No, actually I was at N.A.T.O.," he replied. The North Atlantic Treaty Organization—not exactly a diplomat, but perhaps a secret agent? So very James Bond-esque! Pierce and/or Daniel—could it *really* be true?

Before I let my imagination get the better of me, I rationalized that he was probably just in the military. This was a bit of a red light for me. I wasn't sure if I was much into military men . . . even cute ones. This brought back memories from a few years prior, in a *Princesse J.*-related story, when I'd met another military guy—a bomb diffuser, who tried to court me a little; however, he had been unsuccessful in cracking my code . . . With this news, I didn't know if I should even bother with Dean, but he seemed nice enough. We did have eight hours of general boredom ahead of us . . . It wouldn't hurt to engage in a bit of innocent chatting to pass the time, would it?

"So, what is it exactly you do in the military, Dean?"

"Well, I'm a jet fighter pilot."

—Flight attendants, prepare for takeoff—

A jet fighter pilot? For real? Do they actually exist—I mean, *outside* the movies? Now that I thought of it, he kind of did look like Tom Cruise in *Top Gun.* My interest suddenly skyrocketed. How cool, how dangerous, how terribly *sexy!* He obviously wasn't in uniform or I would have been able to guess his profession from the start, but I could imagine him in one . . . and maybe *without* one, too. I bet jet fighter pilots had to work out a lot; they would have to be able to run fast if their planes were shot down over enemy territory, forcing our poor jet-fighter heroes to parachute into hostile lands . . .

My racy pilot dream was interrupted with another thought—what, then, was he doing in Canada? It turned out that the poor thing was stationed at some remote N.A.T.O. base in the middle of nowhere, but he luckily got to escape from his icy base to occasionally attend meetings at its headquarters in Brussels.

We talked, and laughed, and talked . . . and the hours flew by at Mach speed. We got to know each other better, and after loosening up with a few glasses of wine over our airplane "dinners," the discussion even got a bit intimate. I learned that Dean was in the process of getting divorced (*wince*). Yikes, that meant he would be *très* complicated.

This news launched a tennis match of good features vs. bad ones in my mind. He'd struck many successful points at the beginning, but this latest one balanced out the match. Then came another strike: in addition to the estranged wife, he also had kids—and not just one or two, but FOUR! And all under ten years old! Wife, kids . . . how *old* did all of this make Mr. Jet Fighter Pilot? Was this match going to end at deuce? He turned out to be only 35 (*saved*); he'd certainly managed to keep *busy* when he was on solid ground. No trip home had been spared!

In no time we seemed to be closing in on the North American continent. I had to get a bit of shut-eye as I was going directly to the pre-wedding events from the airport, so I put our potentially endless conversation on hold. It would be picked up again in the near future. He also said that he would be in Europe for work in a few weeks and . . . maybe we could resume it then . . . in person?

The overall idea of Dean was terribly exciting, and he was rather good-looking. As much as I was looking for a passionate summer *amour*, the nitty-gritty facts were clear. The odds of anything really coming out of our meeting were quite minimal. But hey, you never know! I had to keep my romance options open. Maybe he actually traveled a lot and we could meet up in exotic destinations; this particular idea fit the profile of an *aventure* extremely well.

FROM: DEAN L.   Tuesday, April 11 2006 11:33 AM

Hi Lily,
So, how was the wedding? Well, I really enjoyed meeting you on the plane and our "in-depth" discussions! You seem like a fascinating person and . . .

He hadn't wasted any time—I must have stayed on his mind. He got in touch right after our meeting—the first email of many to come. We were separated by 6,000 kilometers (3,700 miles), but not by technology. We e-mailed and Skyped as often as we could. As I said before, our in-flight conversation had touched on some personal issues, especially matters of the heart. Dean was trying to get himself back on his feet after separating from the person he'd thought was "the love of his life," so in a way, he was kind of looking for a little pick-me-up as well.

Throughout our correspondence, we never seemed to have enough time to finish what whatever discussion we had started, so we began a tradition of asking each other three questions to be answered before the next chat:

FROM: DEAN L.   Friday, 21 April 2006 4:42 PM

Dear Lily,

Thanks so much for your lovely letter . . . it's always great to hear from you!
Anyways, thanks for your open and honest answers to the questions! We seem to have very similar notions of a "good" first date and I admire the fact that you have a good idea of which direction you are headed in life. Of course, things can always "pop up" that change our best-laid plans in mid-sentence too . . .
Wow, your questions were tough! Okay, Lily, I'll leave you with these:

1. What "qualities" do you seek in an ideal relationship? Why?

2. How important is the role of physical attraction? At first, and then later?
3. Do you have any pictures you can share?

Soon I'll be making plans to visit Paris on my way to a N.A.T.O. conference. I'm very flexible at this point but was wondering how your schedule looked for a potential visit from May 10-12? Please let me know . . .

"Well, do you want to see him again?" interrogated Naughty cautiously.

"His idea of being quite a fan of theater and the arts is, 'going to see *Les Misérables* and the *Phantom of the Opera?*'" scoffed Pussycat, reading his answers to my previous questions. At least I had the girls to keep me in check.

"It sounds like you're taking part in the *Dating Game* or found each other on some online dating site . . . beware," added Special Kay. She'd recently tried meeting someone through a French dating site, only to go on a hundred first dates (at least she was starting to forget about her boss's evil son). Most of the guys using the site were looking for some quick action, but they were looking in the wrong place: Kay would have none of that.

"What's the harm in some innocent chatting? He may never actually come back," I rationalized, trying to save face.

"Well, he sounds pretty into you . . . and may have other aspirations," warned Naughty. Pussycat and Kay nodded in unison.

There was probably some truth in their observations. While I was happy at the thought of our meeting up again—and for me to realize the full potential of my summer romance quest—I was a little concerned. Who knew what life would throw our way? Perhaps I could be ready for something more serious than the little summer *aventure*—that is, if the right person were to come around. Though I was fond of Dean, I still didn't see how there could be any morsel of a future for us. Was it worth contemplating this dilemma? Or, was I supposed to live in the moment and face these decisions if they came up?

FROM: DEAN L.   Monday, 1 May 2006 5:09 PM

Although I had really hoped to see you in Paris shortly . . . Unfortunately, a few plans changed in my office (a long story!) and now I won't be attending the conference next week. The next trip I know for sure that will bring me back your way will be early June. However, I'm also a fairly spontaneous individual, so if that also gets canceled, I could get the "urge" to just go on a short vacation to the "City of Light" at any time.

You seem like the type of gal who enjoys adventures too? I guess I am the kind of person who likes adventures . . . We only live once!

Tempting . . . this was very, very true. We only live once; but with whom should we spend our precious time?

FROM: DEAN L.   Tuesday, 30 May 2006 8:38 AM

Hey Lily,
So, did you get enough sleep last night? :) Surprisingly, I actually slept great and managed to stay under the covers until about 9 am!
Anyway, I just wanted to tell you that I had a great time last night! Thanks for the wonderful tour of the city and, of course,

> the lovely kisses. :) Needless to say, I'm really looking
> forward to Fri. Hope your week goes well!

So he did come back to Paris, and we did spend a few days together . . . and maybe a few nights, too. Was my summer romance actually going to work out?

Dean had a conference in Belgium, but he'd arranged to fly in and out of Paris so that we could see each other. On his way back to North America, we were going to go somewhere romantic together, to test out some of the amorous philosophies that we'd been discussing in our countless chats. In the meantime, I'd set aside the evening of his arrival in Paris for us to start catching up in person.

It was a gorgeous June evening and I'd chosen the steps of the Opera Garnier as our meeting point, a *très romantique* setting, the marble columns and golden accents being positively regal and fairytale-esque. I was a little nervous as I approached the sparkling, imposing building; we hadn't seen each other in almost two months. What was I getting myself into? Would I even be able to recognize him? I was starting to wonder if this was such a good idea . . . I muted the anxious voice in my mind. I had to live in the moment and just go with it; "we only live once" would have to be my motto for this little *aventure*. I took a deep breath and scouted the crowd of tourists loitering about on the steps. There he was—just as cute as ever.

"Hi Dean, welcome to Paris!" I greeted him with a first kiss . . . on the cheek.

Let the fairytale begin! I kept up the romantic atmosphere, guiding him from the Opera to the elegant Place Vendome: crowned with a column by Emperor Napoleon I, it was home to the Ritz and the top jewelers of the city (and thus absolutely fit for princesses). We crossed over the swanky rue Saint Honoré, lined with its haute couture boutiques, and reached the regal Jardin des Tuileries which were once the gardens of the French royals (again, perfect in keeping with my regal theme!). We meandered along the shady lanes, admiring the delicate mythological statues, eventually coming to a quiet outdoor café, where we stopped to catch up over *apéro*. It was indeed nice to see him in person. His radiant smile was contagious; we laughed and chatted away, our conversation flowing easily from topic to topic.

We carried on our stroll as the sun was lowering to the west, casting beautiful shadows through the peaceful, glowing garden. Our royal path took us through the courtyards of the Louvre Palace, surrounded by the sumptuous former living quarters of the kings and queens. Just nearby we settled on the terrace of one of my favorite cafés, *La Cantine Royal*, for a romantic dinner. Though I didn't agree with all of Dean's points of view, and his slightly conservative perspective, we did have some things in common. He certainly had a strong adventurous side, which would be key to the success (or failure) of our little *aventure*.

After dinner, we pursued our stroll east along the Seine River, which brought us to the Île de la Cité and the queen of all Parisian churches: Notre Dame. The monumental cathedral has been the setting of many torrid French love stories, from Napoleon and Josephine, to Quasimodo and Esmeralda. Was it going to feature in this new romantic tale of mine, too? Admiring it from one of the City of Light's lovely bridges, Dean and I bade each other *bonne nuit* with a few moonlit kisses. Not a bad interlude to our *aventure!*

We would see how the rest of it would unfold the following week.

Dean was in charge of renting a car and I was in charge of the rest. There are so many enchanting places in France to choose from, but in the end I decided on the Loire Valley; it wasn't too far from Paris, and was a great combination of culture, history and natural beauty. The sloping hills of the verdant valley, covered in graceful vineyards, and dotted with turreted castles, were the perfect backdrop for our weekend *aventure*—perhaps the first one of a whole summer filled with fun getaway trips?

The sun was shining brightly as we set off early on Saturday morning, with a first stop in Chartres. No, this was not to have a repeat roll in the hay like I'd had with Julien the shepherd boy—those wheat fields were looking just as prickly as last June. I was after a different kind of loving this summer. We stopped for a quick peek at the famous cathedral and its heavenly stained glass windows before enjoying a lovely lunch with a glass of *rosé* in the historic city center.

We arrived in *La Loire* mid-afternoon, enough time to have a quick perusal of two of the area's finest châteaux: Blois and Amboise. Each one rich in royal history, and perfectly majestic, they certainly amplified the fairytale-like atmosphere of our weekend.

Finishing up our castle visits, we made our way to the quaint 17th-Century manor and B&B that I'd found for us. It wasn't quite a full-fledged château, but was close enough! Perched imposingly on a hill overlooking the Loire River, like many of the official castles, its walls must have hidden equally fascinating stories—if not of princes and princesses, then of modern-day visitors, and we were about to add to the canon!

Similar to many of the châteaux, it had a large garden, but instead of perfectly pruned hedges *à la française*, we found a rather wild *à l'anglaise*-style garden, roamed by exotic chickens, and its more natural design allowed for many discreet areas for picnics and other outdoor adventure sports . . . this suited us just fine for a few reasons . . .

On our way there, we'd stopped at a little shop for some picnic supplies for dinner; the evening was too nice to eat indoors. So after checking in, we went in search of a quiet little grove for our private *dîner*. We spread out a blanket and unpacked our supplies of bread, cheese, strawberries, and a nice bottle of local *Touraine* wine. The wine shed our inhibitions and some of our clothes—and before I knew it, our picnic was getting a little hot and heavy! This might have seemed the perfect chain of events for our romantic weekend; however, our hideout ended up not being all that well-hidden, as the lady of the house spotted us while feeding her flock of chickens! We were caught with our pants down, literally! This made me lose my "appetite," but it didn't seem to bother Dean one bit—it just made him hungrier! Our fable was changing from a sleeping beauty tale into an incestuous Hansel and Gretel story. . . had we left a trail of breadcrumbs back to the house? Would it still be there or might the exotic hens have eaten it up?

The next morning, I attempted to stay clear of an embarrassing run-in with the peeping proprietress; however, she'd laid out a huge breakfast spread (including some odd-looking eggs, probably procured from her multi-breed roost) and acted like she'd witnessed nothing at all the night before. I had to give the French credit for their discretion sometimes!

We started our morning of touring at Villandry castle, especially known for its exceptional gardens, which we *walked* through. I wasn't going to agree to any suggestions from Dean to check out the secluded distant gardens in broad— and public—daylight. We passed by a few other smaller châteaux, eventually calling in at a medieval town for a leisurely lunch beneath a massive towered fortress. Over our meal, we contemplated how we wanted to spend our afternoon. We hadn't really tasted that many local specialties (unless lightly sautéed Canadian *fille* featured on the local menu). While we'd already sipped some regional wine, I realized a visit to an actual vineyard was what our Loire experience was lacking. This became our afternoon mission.

We climbed back in the car and took a road marked "wine route." As we drove along the winding road, we passed many wineries, though they all seemed to be closed. Of course, it was Sunday, the day of rest. Most of France is like a ghost town on Sundays—can't blame the winemakers for following suit. We really should have booked in advance! However, after zigzagging around many winding country roads, we eventually found one that appeared to be open, so we pulled into the driveway to enquire about a tasting.

The house looked quite cute and was reminiscent of the manor we'd stayed at the previous night. While it lacked chickens, there would be some other wildlife that we would gradually meet. Apparently, the charm of the house stopped at the building itself: surrounding it were heaps of junk, empty crates of wine bottles (at least a sign that we were indeed at a vineyard), old run-down cars . . . one of these was barking at us. Ignoring all sensible logic, we left the safety of our rental car.

A woman peered out of the manor's side door. I asked her if it was possible to visit the vineyard or have a tasting. She gave a vague head gesture and disappeared back inside, which I took to be a "yes." The barking van continued barking, heightening my doubts about the place. Well, we were already out of the car and at least they were willing to give us a tour. After a few minutes the manor door reopened and out stepped a middle-aged man who looked more like pig farmer than a winemaker, but who was I to make fashion calls? We were in the countryside after all, and I think we'd also woken him from his post-Sunday-lunch nap. Nevertheless, he strolled over to us with a big smile and introduced himself as Maurice. He then went over to the barking van. I clung to Dean's arm, bracing myself for a herd of gigantic, vicious German Shepherds, only to be greeted by two of the cutest and friendliest puppies in the Loire. They came bouncing over and attacked us with enthusiastic jumps and licks. Seeing how excited the pups were (probably because they'd been freed from their over-heated van prison), Maurice said he would have offered to let us take one of them home, but they were already spoken for. They become our instant new friends and energetic shadows.

Maurice said he'd take us on the full tour. Once again, I don't think we knew what we were in for. Off he headed through the grape vines, a graceful contrast to the scruffy winemaker, in his dirt-smeared coveralls and not so sexy days-old stubble. Off we went after him, our furry friends close behind. Maurice started down a lowered path leading to an old doorway—here, beneath the vines, was his very authentic wine *cave*.

Following the pups and Maurice inside, we found a cavern

of moldy wine barrels, vintage dates roughly scribbled on their sides. The casual Maurice started to explain his different *Bourgueil* A.O.C. wines, while I translated for Dean. He grabbed a few glasses from a nearby box and uncorked the large barrels one by one, directly acquiring samples with a sort of glass siphon—all indicators that this was indeed a real tasting (he even gave some to the puppies, directly into their mouths from the same siphon he used for our glasses!).

After about 20 minutes, we resurfaced to the warm sunny fields. But the visit didn't end there—Maurice proceeded to take us to his tasting room. I'd been to a good many vineyards in France. Usually the tasting room is tidy and nicely decorated, ready for unexpected visits . . . this was not the case here. We entered a dark room covered with dusty, disheveled boxes of sampling glasses and crates of empty wine bottles. Maurice brushed off the table with a ratty old newspaper, beckoning us to sit while he whipped out three glasses and few bottles of different wines.

We all got a little tipsy while tasting the various wines and laughing over funny cultural topics, so much so that I feared we would end up staying for dinner if I didn't come up with an escape route. I tried for an easy out by buying a few cases of wine. While paying in the back office, I heard a distinct *baaaah*. Maurice, keenly observing the puzzled look on my face, confirmed that I'd heard correctly—there were indeed goats out back, and now he would just have to introduce us to them.

Maurice had been given temporary guardianship of two adorable baby dwarf goats. He was telling us in minute detail the whole story of how he'd ended up with them, when suddenly he was struck with an ingenious idea. He couldn't offer me one of the puppies, but he claimed that dwarf goats were currently all the rage in Paris. *Goats? In Paris?* We really had to insist on leaving before we found ourselves with a smelly goat in the back seat of our rental car, bleating and nibbling at our hair all the way back to Paris. But as we were edging towards the car, Maurice had another sudden brainwave. With much enthusiasm, he exclaimed that he absolutely had to show us the frescoes. *The frescoes?* Oh yes, he had some secret cultural patrimony adorning the walls of his ancient demure. This visit was really turning into more than we had bargained for.

Our goat-herding winemaker led us over to the manor tower, and up we went to the attic. Heaving open the heavy door, we emerged into a large, musty loft littered with miscellaneous garbage, old record players, and a graveyard of abandoned bed frames. Above the chaotic mass of clutter were, as he had promised, the delicate remains of 15th-Century landscape paintings. My vinous haze transported my mind back to when this probably had been quite the splendid estate, where a lovely princess might have lived with her *prince charmant.* My mental mirage was interrupted by Maurice asking me if I thought he could get money from the government to preserve them. This was getting to be a little too much; my fairytale escape was going to end up with me riding off into the sunset on a dwarf goat led by the wrong prince charming. We had to get out of there! I had to admit our little wine adventure wasn't exactly what I'd planned on, but it was certainly an adventure.

As we drove further away from the magical land of châteaux and closer to Paris, our fable was gradually coming to a close . . . but what would this tale have a happy ending?

Dean gently clasped my hand, gave me a tender look and asked; "So what about us . . .?" *What about us . . .? What do you mean—who's this "us"?* Well, we'd left the goat back in the Loire . . . sure, we had many bottles of wine in the trunk, but I didn't think he was referring to stocking an impressive wine cellar. I guess the "us" had to be *Dean + me.*

I'd come to the gradual realization that this prince was meant for someone else. It was sweet that he would even consider an "us" . . . but firstly, although I was looking for more than a flighty fling this summer, I wasn't looking for an "us." Secondly, I was pretty sure that I wouldn't want to be the second half of an "us" with Dean, given the circumstances. What options were there? He didn't really know when he'd be back in Europe, so the summer romance options were looking pretty bleak. Hypothetically, we could try to keep up a ridiculous long distance "real" relationship (but how long could that last?). Or would I have to give up Paris (my city!) and move to some military base, only to become a housewife, a step-mom straight from *Cinderella?* Dean might be able to get himself a permanent transfer to N.A.T.O., but even in that best possible scenario, what was I to do? Commute back and forth between Paris and Brussels? Maybe the US would invade France; then he could come over for good with his fighter jet! Honestly, the latter seemed the most feasible possibility.

Finally, logistical factors aside, another point arose, which was even more important in the "us" equation: as much as I'd had a nice (enough) weekend, I'd been putting on a sort of sunny charade and even after getting to know him, I didn't think there was really *je t'aime* with Dean; I couldn't see myself building anything concrete with him. Dean just wasn't my type. He was adventurous, cute, kind and romantic, but in many other regards we were just on different planets, or in this case, kingdoms.

We bid each other a fond farewell in front of the Château Rouge *métro* station (a world away from the romance of castle country), with promises to stay in touch, but no other serious declarations. A jet fighter pilot had all the allure to make for an exciting summer adventure, but this one just wasn't going to take off. The summer was about to officially begin; I'd better get my tickets in order or I might just miss the *je t'aime* plane . . . again.

FROM: JAKE   Friday, 9 June 2006 11:41 AM

Hi Lily,
Good to bump into you the other night. Hope the concert was good. You certainly looked very happy to be going there, though you usually look pretty happy to be going most places. Is that a Canadian thing?

Le Rendez-vous des amis

DAVE [06/10/06 6:33 PM]
It's too nice an evening to stay inside,
care for a drink at the usual?

"Weren't you looking for someone sweet and fun?"

"Yes, well, yes and no . . ."

"You can't be so indecisive. You were playing with the poor pilot's heartstrings."

"*Me?* Playing with his heartstrings? Dave, need I remind you that he's the one who said he was looking for a little adventure . . ."

"Couldn't you see that he was growing attached? It seems rather plain and simple from how you described his emails."

"Don't forget about his job. Would you like to see me disappear into military oblivion? Never to be seen off of a military base?"

"You might be exaggerating a tad there, but you do have a point. I don't know what I would do if you left Paris . . ."

We were getting into dangerous territory here and just as I was about to talk about the warm weather, Dave pushed on:

"Didn't you realize from this experience that it was good

to date an Anglophone . . . maybe you should give it more of a try, but with someone based here?"

"Actually—No! I don't know what to think anymore, as I obviously don't know North American dating codes anymore. Maybe I need to go back to trying someone French?"

"Or perhaps, someone who's half-and-half? Best of both worlds . . .?"

Oh jeez, here we go again! I needed to find a good romance candidate ASAP before Dave actually had legitimate grounds to fill the position!

Summer Romance Resolutions - June

- Give a second thought to all this nationality distinction . . . there must be better criteria out there to find my perfect summer romance candidate

- Along a similar vein, don't assume that if you speak the same language you will actually be on the same wavelength!

- Try to find out ASAP if candidate is:

  - recently divorced

  - (if so) looking for a second/third/fourth wife

  - in the military

  - living across the world

- Attempt to sit beside quiet old lady on planes . . . much safer than cute young man

- If you come across baby goats or barking vans, back away and run in the opposite direction as quickly as possible

- Don't forget: châteaux do not guarantee fairytale love stories

TERRIBLI FOXY!

FOXY [06/25/06 03:43 AM]
Good night my Tigresse! Big kiss.
I am terribli sorry for tonight! I wait
tomorrow. Have a good dream.

*—Hi Lily, I know it's last minute, but if you're free tonight,
I'm having a party at my office with clients and students.
It would be great if you could come!—*

This was a voicemail message from a colleague at one of the language schools I occasionally worked for. *Hmmm* . . . It was a beautiful summer Friday night and I hadn't made any plans yet; I might as well go along to the party.

I put on a cute summery dress and touched up my makeup, yet didn't make too much of a fuss; most of the students and colleagues from that school were older, and/or married with kids, so while they were fun, I doubted there would necessarily be anyone in attendance to impress. That said, as I have discovered, one must always be ready for the unexpected!

When I turned down the little street not far from the Canal Saint Martin, I found a surprising bustling mass of people of all ages. I said some quick hellos and helped myself to the wonderful Indian buffet which was full of tasty veggie treats, and complemented it all with a chilled *rosé*.

Vive the start of summer! I was having a fabulous time chatting with some other colleagues and a few former students whom I hadn't seen in a while. Maybe it had been a good idea to come after all?

"Where is that Foxy, he's always late!" exclaimed one of the lady students I was talking to, as she checked her phone for messages.

Foxy . . .? Hmmm, I liked the sound of him already. "Who's Foxy?" I asked, my curiosity getting the better of me.

"Oh, you've never had Foxy in your class?" responded the student, coyly. "He's a riot; you're going to love him!"

There are times when you hear talk about a certain *monsieur,* or see him for the first time, that you immediately know something is destined to happen with him. There's this spark that ignites and there's no stopping it (sort of like what had happened with Mario—don't forget, fire can also be very dangerous!). I got the sense that, more than anything, I would find out personally that this Foxy character would stand true to his nickname.

"Hey *girrrrls!!* I'm here!" Speak of the devil . . . I wasn't disappointed in the slightest when I met Foxy in the flesh. Cute and confident, he had a killer smile, short blond hair and fiery green eyes that could melt any delicate heart. Our respective green eyes met, and brief introductions were made before he bounced off to greet everyone. He spent more time chatting with his former fellow classmates, most of them girls, but I subtly kept my eye on him.

As the clock ticked onward and the stars grew in number, the party-attendees progressively drifted away, leaving behind the fun ones. Would we simply end our pleasant night then and there?

"Why don't we go to the *Bordela Braziliana*? It's just around the corner," someone suggested. *Oh God*, I hadn't been there since that fateful night back in March. However, ever since, I'd harbored the secret hope of running into Keanu again; this could be my lucky night. So, I eagerly, though nervously, tagged along.

We made it past the door's tough bouncer fairly easily, and even managed to score a section of one of the *Bordela*'s long picnic-like tables. Soon the atmosphere picked up, we enjoyed a few more drinks (no vodka shots!), and up we climbed onto the tables to dance.

Since we'd left the party, Foxy had been paying more attention to me and the flirting level was on the rise. He definitely seemed like excellent *aventure* material. Maybe I could make up for Dean's non-compatibility; Foxy definitely seemed more cool and fun-loving . . . plus, it was just the beginning of summer, and thus time for the love thermostat to rise.

Foxy started moving closer and closer to me . . . would he make a move? Now we were dancing right next to each other, and I could feel his foxy vibes. In spite of this, I began to notice that he very suspiciously kept checking his phone, contradicting his 'going for a home run' behavior. Then, virtually out of nowhere, this other girl showed up, full of smiles, and kissed Foxy on the cheek. *Hmmpf!* That— or rather *she*—wasn't part of the plan! It turned out that there might be a little curveball in this new round of potential summer romance, but I wasn't going to drop the ball.

Who was this *petite française*? I sized up the competition.

She was younger than I was and a tad cute in a provincial sort of way, but I beat her in the sexiness department, and I couldn't help think there really seemed to be more fire between Foxy and me. I did sense that he was a bit of a player, but after the more seriously-inclined Dean, I didn't mind if my summer romance was slightly on the light and fluffy side—it just needed to last through the summer! So, I was ready to go in swinging to the battle for Foxy. He would dance a bit with me, and when he saw the other girl getting a bit jealous he would go spend time with her. I'd been willing to play hard-ball, but I didn't know what to make of all this. As the night went on, I gradually stopped caring too much as to whether I'd win him or not. Besides, there had to be other strike-out pitchers in the *Bordela Ballpark*, so I decided to go scouting on the dance floor and get away from the tangled love triangle that was forming.

I scanned the dancing crowd, hoping to catch a glimpse of Keanu (and NOT Bad Blair). Neither of them was in sight. Oh well, I could always drag the girls out another night to come fishing for Keanu.

Working my way back to our table through the sea of sweaty dancers, I was suddenly yanked from their midst into a dark corner. Before I could realize what was happening, I was being ferociously kissed by my kidnapper! *Who would dare?* Was it Blair? . . . Keanu? *Mais non*, it was Mr. Foxy!

"I've been dying to kiss you all night!" he declared, once we'd torn ourselves from the passionate embrace. "It's a complicated situation. You see, I promised to go out with this other girl tonight. We met at a party recently and she came into Paris especially to see me. I can't let her down, but I'd rather be with you!"

Hmmpf was right! It certainly was a complicated and unexpected twist to my evening. After his fiery kiss and explanation of his "situation," I couldn't bear going back to the table and seeing them dance together while being shot the evil eye by the competition. So, numbers and promises to see each other were fervently exchanged, and a farewell kiss was savored in our secret corner before I headed out . . . alone— but I hadn't struck out. I was anxious to know when our rematch would be. Had I finally found my flaming summer passion? Just as I was crawling into bed, I got this message:

FOXY [06/25/06 03:43 AM]

Good night my Tigresse! Big kiss.
I am terribli sorry for tonight! I wait
tomorrow. Have a good dream.

It seemed like I really *would* see this Foxy again. His English spelling might not have been strong, but never mind. One thing was for sure; I would definitely "have a good dream" with images of *terribli* Foxy lingering in my head.

Foxy did contact me the next day, and we fixed a date to meet up two days later, on a Monday. I didn't have to work on the Tuesday, so it was perfect. We *rendezvous*-ed at his place (I know, I know; I'd sort of scrapped that resolution last year, but we were already in summer, no time to lose!). The address he gave me was across town, in the 15th district, a rather residential part of the city. It was not exactly party central, so I was surprised to find Foxy living there, but maybe he liked a little tranquility after late-night madness. On my trek over there, my excitement picked up: this could be it! Foxy was the ideal contender for the right, light summer romance I needed. Even though I hadn't quizzed him in regards to my resolution factors, things seemed to be headed on the right track.

After an incredibly *chaud* welcome greeting, we managed to detach from each other and Foxy prepared some icy drinks to cool us down (he was a much better host than some *men* I've known . . .especially the Spanish ones!). Looking around the place, the antique furniture, lace doilies, porcelain figurines and musty smell gave me the distinct impression that I was not in a "young partier's" apartment.

"Oh, this is my mother's home," Foxy said, probably noting the bemused look on my face as I scanned the room. "I'm just staying with her for a bit. She's on holiday this week. I won't be here long, though."

"Why not? Are you moving into your own place?"

"No, I'm going to Manchester!"

"*Manchester?* When are you going to Manchester?"

"July tenth." *What?* That was in less than two weeks! Now I truly saw the importance of going over my resolution questions *before* accepting invitations, not after! Okay, I had to calm down and stop jumping to conclusions—*maybe he wasn't staying for long?*

"What are you doing in Manchester?" I forced myself to ask.

"I'm doing a three-month intensive English course to get me ready for my trip!"

"Your trip? Where are you going?" *Uh-oh, things were going from bad to worse!*

"To Australia! To work for one year! I'm so excited!"

Australia! Now that was much, much further away than Manchester. He might have been very excited about his plans, but I definitely wasn't. How could Foxy be my summer romance if he was leaving? I wanted something to last the whole summer, but was a ten-day summer *aventure* better than no summer loving (especially if it's with a fun, super sexy guy)? But before I had time to come to an answer, I was being ferociously kissed on the sofa, which conveniently turned into a bed, which turned into the next morning.

Foxy was indeed incredibly sexy . . . and incredibly passionate. I knew that he was not the kind of guy I would actually want to have a serious relationship with. While I liked to have fun, he was an absolute party animal, and I doubted he had much ambition (at this stage in his life) for things besides finding the best soirées to go to or the right guest lists to get on. He seemed more interested in World Cup soccer (which was currently taking place) than world peace. But passion is passion, and the red-hot flame between us would not be extinguished until he left for Manchester. We saw a fair amount of each other in the short time frame, and while I think he went out for wild and crazy partying almost every other night when we weren't together, from his affection and frequent messages I was pretty sure he didn't have other girls on the go:

FOXY [07/30/06 05:53 AM]

I'm just getting home! Thinking of you,
big kiss and have a nice day

Even though his messages were at odd hours of the day (or rather, the morning), at least he was thinking of me . . . and thus (most probably) not in the arms of another *fille*. It was nice to have the perfectly measured amount of attention; Foxy was French after all, and most French men are really attentive . . . when they want to be. If you've hooked them in, you can be showered with adoration and sweet messages, even if they are temporary.

FOXY [07/03/06 07:04 AM]

A little hello to wish you a good day.
Another little night of craziness. Big kiss

He made some time for me in and around his other nights of mayhem. One of the nicest times we spent together was on an extended lunch date. It was a beautiful sunny day, and Foxy said he wanted to take me to a special restaurant. My eyes must have lit up with childish glee at his romantic invitation, before converting into fear—*I hope this place serves something vegetarian.* I would just have to wait and see.

Arriving on a little street just off from the Seine, near Saint Michel, I realized that we were going to one of the oldest restaurants in Paris, one that I'd walked past dozens of times and had always dreamed of dining at. I would have double the luck, because they weren't too busy, so we were seated on a little flower-covered balcony ledge, which we had all to ourselves. It was like our own private restaurant! As such, our "personal chef" prepared some appetizing vegetarian options for me. It was bliss! We nibbled on culinary delicacies, sipped mouthwatering wine, and enjoyed enough laughter to fill us for days.

After our leisurely lunch, we strolled the short distance down to the river and spent the rest of the afternoon snuggled together on a sunny piece of grass by the Seine. This was exactly what a summer romance was supposed to be like . . . I avoided thinking of the end, and chose instead to savor the moment while it lasted.

A few days later, his mom came back from holidays and Foxy introduced us over an *apéro* at her/their place. I think she began to take a liking to me (she might not have had a chance to meet many of his other *filles*); however, she wouldn't have enough time to get to really like me. We then went out to watch a World Cup soccer match and—bizarrely enough for an un-athletically-inclined gal like me—I actually found it kind of fun (were Foxy and his ways rubbing off on me?). France was doing well and heading for the finals, though I was sort of sad to think that there wouldn't be a fun season for Foxy and I, no grand victory in the finals for us. Manchester was calling . . .

Why couldn't Foxy stay just a little (tiny, itsy bit) longer? He didn't need to go to gray Manchester to improve his English—he could improve it right here in Paris with me; with my experience, I'd be the best personal teacher he could ever have! Surely the language of love was the most efficient way to learn?

And so ended the best attempt I'd had at a summer fling or romance since beginning my quest the previous year. I was in mild despair. *I'd gotten so close!* There was almost enough *je t'aime*. Summer was just getting started and my flame was starting to burn brighter; but, who could keep the momentum going?

SILVAIN [07/06/06 11:57 PM]
I hope you've planned a little evening
for me this week in your busy agenda . .
unless you've forgotten me!

fermé le 7 juillet en raison du coupe de monde de football, retrouvez-nous pour le match final au café-tabac à côté !

(closed due to soccer World Cup, join us at café next door to watch the final match!)

DAVE [07/07/06 7:18 PM]
Shame about the World Cup closure,
will I see you soon anyway?

Summer Romance Resolutions - July

Follow previous resolutions, but before any
of the other items:

ASK POTENTIAL FLING CANDIDATE IF HE
WILL ACTUALLY BE IN PARIS FOR THE
SUMMER!

LE GOÛT DES AUTRES

FROM: JEAN-CLAUDE T. Tuesday, June 20, 2006 4:44 PM

So, it will be when you want, where you want, how you want
. . . but with me.

Foxy was like a deep-sea earthquake that would set in
motion one turbulent, summer-long romantic tsunami. The
timing was so tumultuous that it's hard to put everything in
order; nonetheless, I suppose Jean-Claude belongs right after
Foxy . . . as his polar opposite.

Little Foxy was the exception to the rule, but in general,
my job didn't offer too many possibilities for suitable
romantic encounters. As the younger French were learning
English more efficiently at school than in days gone by, my
students were predominantly middle-aged, (married) men.

There is a French movie called *Le Goût des Autres*,
translated as "The Taste of Others," directed by Agnès Jaoui.
In this case, 'Taste' refers to interest, not taste buds, but now
that I think about it, maybe it does include a little of both.

In the film, one of the main characters falls in love with his English teacher. This kind of thing doesn't only happen in the movies: I'd heard about real life stories of the same situation . . . and I was about to find myself in the thick of a similar plot.

We have to rewind a few months to March, when I started teaching an important senior director at a very large French company. Jean-Claude was a distinguished, fairly attractive man in his early 50s. His English wasn't very good, but he preferred to focus on practicing his speaking skills rather than doing grammar or boring lessons on mergers and acquisitions (maybe because he didn't need any help with *those* tactics?). Our conversations inevitably led to discussing his personal life and interests. He didn't talk about too many private topics like some people did (I ended up being a sort of psychiatrist), but he spoke a fair amount about two of his passions: sailing and traveling.

Jean-Claude was always very discreet and never openly flirted or tried slipping sly seductive comments into our discussions. However, when he started insisting that I really had to visit the northern French coastline and that he would be *more* than happy to take me, suspicions alarm bells started going off in my head—but by then it was already too late! Summer was fast approaching, and it was already promising to be a hot one! His invitation to "have a class" outside Paris wasn't an easy one to avoid, though one I should have declined immediately. My country Canadian *naïveté* can get the better of me sometimes . . . nevertheless, I wasn't about to go away for the whole weekend with him!

FROM: JEAN-CLAUDE T.   Tuesday, June 20, 2006 4:44 PM

Hi Lily,

It's a pity, but . . . I'll go where you want, east, west, north, south, inside, outside, upside, downside, side by side, but not offside. Seriously, if we have only one day, I propose to go to Normandy, I suppose you know Honfleur, Trouville, Deauville or not? What do you prefer, or something else?

How was I going to get out of this one? In the end, I compromised, reducing his weekend invitation to a day trip somewhere nearby. Could a little day excursion to Normandy really hurt?

Normandy: land of cider, Camembert cheese . . . and conquests (I think we can guess which of the three Jean-Claude had in mind!). It's a lovely region spanning from the northwest of Paris through to the English Channel. Many Parisians have a second home in one of the quaint villages nestled in the rolling hills of the area, in between cows and castle ruins. It really was a picture postcard of France. Yet, it had a troublesome battle-related history featuring two important conquests. First, there was the Normans' conquest of England, leading to their victory at the Battle of Hastings in 1066. Then, almost a millennium later, the victories were reversed at D-Day, with the allies coming from the north to attack German-occupied France in 1944.

I thought our day was going to be a casual trip to see a couple of old fortresses from the early Norman era with a light lunch along the way. If only I had sensed the conquering undertones of his destination choice, I might have been able to plan for a better defense. Jean-Claude as was prepared as the allied forces for his attempted conquest . . .

Our D-Day arrived, and unlike the turbulent weather of the historic event, it was bright and sunny, ideal visibility for an attack. We *rendezvous*ed outside a *métro* station on the outskirts of the city and off we drove westward. The morning passed without incident: we innocently stopped to visit a little Norman village with quaint half-timbered houses and an abandoned mill: the perfect scenery for an idyllic 19th-Century landscape painting.

Then, around noon we pulled over at a charming *auberge*, nestled in another picturesque, sleepy town just up the road. *What were we doing here?* This was his carefully chosen Michelin-starred lunch restaurant. Dread crept over me. Due to the extreme heat, I was wearing a tank top and linen skirt: nice enough, but hardly adequate attire for an elegant lunch. That wasn't even the worst of it. It was a very fancy, very French restaurant . . . which meant that there would be nothing vegetarian in sight! What was I going to be able to eat? At some point in all of our conversations, I was certain I'd already mentioned to Jean-Claude that I was a vegetarian; however, it must have slipped his obviously one-track mind. What a terrible bind I was in; I knew that he was only trying to impress (or more and more apparently, to seduce) me, and I didn't want to disappoint him or make things uncomfortable by asking them to make me something special. But could I really manage to eat . . . *meat?* In the split second I had to decide, I felt obliged to grin and bear it.

I hadn't intentionally eaten any meat, chicken or seafood in over a decade. There had been, of course, a few mishaps, such as Italian grandmas including some bacon in a dish "just for flavor," or choosing the wrong sort of mystery canapés at cocktail parties, but I was otherwise quite strict on the matter. Even though I didn't relish the idea of going against my principles, I decided I could use this awkward (and potentially palate offensive) situation as a test, to make sure I really still wanted to stay a vegetarian, which was a serious challenge in meat-loving France. Maybe easing-up on my personal rules by including fish would make my life easier?

Contemplating the minimal, but refined list of summer specials, I scanned for the least awful option. I ordered some grilled trout with apple risotto, hoping that I could have a bite or two and then discreetly mask the *pauvre poisson* under some lettuce. After meekly placing my order, I took a deep breath—and a large sip of my champagne—it couldn't be that bad, could it? Oh yes, it could!

I tried to hide the desperation on my face when the waiter carefully placed my main course down in front of me. *What was I going to do?* As this was a high-end place, there was not a shred of greenery on my plate! Well, except for some decorative parsley, but that could hardly help my cause! So I had to—slowly and painfully—eat the greater part of the sad, little, dead trout . . . Thank goodness there was champagne to wash it down. Such a lunch would normally have been a strategic advance, but the meal had definitely not helped win me over.

I was fairly eager to end this somewhat traumatic two-hour meal and get on with our little day-trip. Finally, Jean-Claude asked for the bill and we would be on our way. If only things could have been so simple!

"Since we are here, it would be nice to visit some of your rooms," Jean-Claude requested to the Maître D'.

"*Bien sûr*, Monsieur."

I'd managed to make it through lunch without any romantic advances, but I realized I was totally in for it now. *Why did he want to see the rooms?* Luckily, the Maître D' accompanied us through the series of cozy love dens and I wasn't left all alone with Jean-Claude.

As the door to the first room swung open, my wishful student was very taken.

"This one is so nice, and let's see . . . what a romantic view from the window . . ." My thoughts were far from his! *Oh my God! Au secours! Could some divinity* (Greek, Mayan, Norse Viking) *or hero* (i.e. those who saved Private Ryan—I was in no position to be picky) *please save me from being held as a love hostage in this Norman hamlet?* I called out this barrage of thoughts in my mind—and thus to empty ears.

I couldn't bear to set foot inside the room. Off we paraded to love shack #2. As the Maître D' gently opened the door, Jean Claude let out a gasp: "This one might be even cozier . . . I could almost settle into the bed right now!"

Before he attempted to fulfill his desires, I yelped, "Yes, it's certainly cute . . . but look! It seems like there's a cow stuck in the windmill at the river; maybe we should go for help!" and slipped out of the room on a rescue mission of my *own* personal safety. Yikes! That was a close call. What exactly did he have in mind for this little excursion? An intimate lesson in English pillow talk?

Managing to leave the *auberge* safe and sound, I let my guard down a little; the coast was now clear of any bedrooms. Nevertheless, here I was in the middle of nowhere in Normandy, with only cows and dangerous windmills to assist me as an excuse to escape the situation, leagues away from Paris or any means of getting there. So, I figured the best thing to do was to take it easy and try to enjoy the rest of our drive. What was the worst that could happen? He wouldn't actually try anything . . . *would he?*

Next stop was a medieval hilltop fortress, where we had a nice chat about the history of the region; it was good to change the subject from *auberges*, though the topic of the Normans' skills at <u>conquest</u> did slightly put me back on alert. After the castle tour (which thankfully involved no dungeons or towers for maidens to be locked up in), we strolled through the new town. Somehow, once again, the path led to another cute inn with a great restaurant. I wasn't about to repeat our lunch experience twice in one day! Those Norse gods pulled through this time: it was (luckily) closed, and owing to Jean-Claude's dismay, we were forced to sip a refreshing drink at a normal café, free of any rooms for rent.

Back in the car, we headed towards Giverny, the destination I was most keenly looking forward to. Claude Monet had planted himself and thousands of flowers here, unknowingly putting the village on the tourist map. As an art lover, I was thrilled to be able to see the place that so greatly inspired the gifted Impressionist. Alas, when we arrived, they were closing up for the day, and I was only able to catch a quick glimpse as we passed by. Jean-Claude didn't seem to mind too much that the Monet Foundation was closed; I soon realized why he'd chosen to include Giverny. As peaceful and as tranquil as the hamlet seemed, it was a minefield of little B&Bs! And Jean-Claude pointed out each and every one.

"Wouldn't it be nice to stay there . . . so romantic! Look at that one: the perfect lovers' getaway!"

Sure, they were romantic, but it would depend on *whom*

you were with! As I was not falling for his bait, he glumly got back on the road to Paris. *Whew,* I'd almost made it through the day; we were in the final stretch, nearing home base. But Jean-Claude wasn't going to miss out on this opportunity at conquest. It was now or never.

"I have to tell you something." *Oh dear . . .* I was trying not to think of the worst possible scenario. I had to stay positive; maybe he was going to suggest I go out with his 24-year-old son?

For him, the English lesson of the day was over, and he switched back into French to give me a little lesson in the language of French love. He could hold back no longer—he had a declaration to make. It had been a *coup de foudre* when he first met me. The lightning bolts of *love at first sight.* Though lightning bolts are, by nature unidirectional, from the sky to their target. And I definitely hadn't been struck by the same bolt. Poor Jean-Claude had been waiting for his turn to strike back.

With his perfect French subtlety, he was indirectly asking if I would become his mistress. As with many Frenchmen of his age, he would inevitably stay married to the same woman forever, all the while pursing other romantic . . . exploits. Having a mistress was okay in his books, almost normal. Well, it was absolutely _not_ okay in mine! Nevertheless, what could I really do at that very moment? Here I was, stuck in a car driving along the highway while Jean-Claude was busy declaring his love and gazing at me, rather than focusing on the road ahead of us. What would save me and get me back to Paris . . . *alive?* I was his prisoner of unrequited love! I tried getting out of this battle skirmish by pointing out the obvious: 'aren't you married?' and 'what about your wife?'

These questions didn't get me out of this deadlock: he merely said that I was being an "American puritan," that my line of thinking was only *one* way of viewing these things. While I didn't agree with this in the slightest, I was out of maneuvers. All I could manage in reply—to put an end to this losing struggle—was that I would think about it.

I would think about it? That was the *wrooong* answer— he took it pretty much as a yes, and snatched up my hand, kissing and squeezing it with all his loving might. Oh God, I'd unleashed a love monster! Was it too late to retract my "maybe"?

The rest of the journey back to Paris was terribly awkward, these sentiments echoed above us as the sunny sky gradually filled with dark gray clouds. He clutched my hand the whole time and kept shooting me adoring looks. I wanted to get out of his car as soon as we hit the first *métro* station, but he insisted on driving me *alllll* the way home. At least I had plans for that evening, and I was already running late, so there was no way he could keep me in his grasp for any longer. As we drove the long way up the Montmartre hill, the clouds opened and down came thick sheets of rain— the wrath of the gods in response to our doomed trip?

I scurried inside and changed into a new outfit, attempting to shed the bad vibes of my bizarre day. Then it was off to meet the girls, dodging lightning bolts and the downpour along the way.

"You said *what?*" screeched Naughty.

"I said I would think about it . . ." I managed to repeat, then shielded myself from an inevitable verbal lashing.

"Think about WHAT?" Naughty was totally against cheating.

"Don't worry, Naughty, I'm NOT going to think about it—I just didn't know what to say in the situation. How else was I supposed to get back to Paris . . . alive?"

She gave me her famous doubtful raised eyebrow and I grabbed another two cocktails off the meandering waiter's tray. I would need a few more of those to forget about my day.

Here we were, four sexy girls out for ladies night. The weekly ladies' evening at a famous club off the *Champs Elysées* was a sneaky ploy to get girls drunk and horny before letting a stampede of 'bulls' in later on, so we usually left when the free drinks stopped being served. How could we ever find suitable romantic matches in such a place? I temporarily pushed my woes to the back of my mind with the help of another icy kamikaze. The lights dimmed, signaling the start of the "ladies show" and out came a sexy, masked commando; maybe he could help save the day?

This latest escapade wasn't in line with my quest at all. Sure, I wanted someone who would actually stick around and also someone more mature than Foxy—but not necessarily more mature in **AGE.** Why had Foxy gone and abandoned me? He would have been the perfect excuse to decline Jean-Claude's advances, had he not left. I was such a bad liar, I couldn't just invent a fake boyfriend.

Jean-Claude was genuinely sweet and charming, but becoming the mistress of a 50-something married businessman, who also had children practically my age, wasn't exactly what I'd had in mind when looking for a romance or even a fling. I sometimes joked that if he'd been the C.E.O. of the company and had his own private jet to fly me around the world on exotic getaways, then I just *might* have considered his proposal (I would later regret making such a declaration, for the opportunity actually came up . . . but that story will have to wait for the next book). This whole story was a definite *je ne t'aime pas.*

My "I'll think about it" only led me to spending the rest of the six months of our lessons evading the subject as best I could, but also involved several a few more fish-filled lunches and attempted kisses.

And so, I tried to get my search for that summer romance back on track. Why couldn't I just find a happy *je t'aime* medium? Someone fun enough, not too old, who would stick around for at least a little while, and most importantly from this last experience—wasn't married!

AUGUST [07/27/06 5.16 PM]
Hey there, I haven't forgotten u
call me when you want kiss

DAVE [08/29/06 6:48 PM]
Le RDV is open again. Care for a
drink? Would love to see you . . .

"Remember our little talk about polygamy?"

"How could I forget? Just because a certain amount of French men think it's acceptable, it doesn't mean it actually is!"

"Poor guy, I feel sorry for him."

"Sorry for *him*? You should feel sorry for his wife! You never know how many times he's tried the same thing."

"You don't even know his wife's perspective. Maybe she has her own young lover?"

I raised an eyebrow, as this was highly doubtful though, I supposed, not totally out of the question. France was home to the largest proportion of swingers clubs per capita . . . but still, it might also have one of the highest percentages of adultery, and I don't think there would be accurate statistics on that.

"You could have given him a try. Men of a certain age can

be more tender, more generous, more experienced in life and lovemak . . ."

"Dave! It was completely out of the question. And besides, I wasn't even attracted to him, so I really didn't see what there would have been in it for me . . . other than sailing weekends in Brittany coupled with expensive fish-filled dinners!"

"Still, I think you need someone more mature, someone who might understand you better, somebody like m. . ."

"I think it's about time I get going home—*now.*"

Summer Romance Resolutions – August/September

- Avoid any work-related romances

- Try to catch early signs of flirting by students and invent wonderful dreamy boyfriend and slip him into conversation every chance you have

- Be wary of any invitations to leave Paris for any reason (should have learned this from the past!)

- Try to bring up the following themes discreetly in conversation:

    - the unacceptability of extramarital affairs

    - my exclusively dating _unmarried_ men and certainly NOT anyone with children over 20 years old

    - vegetarianism, and that fish are not a part of this movement

    - a new proneness to seasickness

- Add "Non, merci" or "Non, ce n'est pas possible" to vocabulary repertoire—erase "I'll think about it."

A LITTLE BIT OF EVILING ANYONE?

JAKE [06/16/06 12:39 AM]
Eviling, I like the new word.
Eviling itself is great too,
as is naughtification.

Okay, besides my other resolutions, I had to come to the conclusion that I wasn't going to meet my perfect "happy medium" summer romance at/on:

a) a salsa club/cafe/bar/dance club

b) country parties, country excursions or anywhere outside of Paris

c) picnics/outdoor cinema events

d) airplanes

e) miscellaneous work situations

What was left?

FROM: JAKE   Friday, 2 June 2006 11:41 AM

Hi Lily, Good to bump into you the other night. Hope the concert was good, you certainly looked very happy to be going there. Though you usually look pretty happy to be going most places. Is that a Canadian thing?

Hmmm, had the winds of fate blown the right candidate my way?

I'd always thought it would be idyllically romantic to meet someone on the *métro*. Okay, the Parisian subway can be a little grimy and smelly, but for me it still had a certain seductive charm. I'd imagined my *rapturous* run-in as something like this:

Mid-afternoon, when the *métro* is not too busy, I get on the train and make my way to a section of four seats. The outside two are already taken, so when I go to sit down in the seat beside the window, my knees gently brush against those of the (sexy, artsy, somewhat tousled) boy sitting on one of the outside seats. The knee-brushing incident would cause him look up to see whose knee had invaded his personal space, only to find cute me in a just-above-the-knee skirt, sitting diagonally across from him. He sneaks a glance at me now and then when he thinks I'm not looking his way. Even though I find him completely irresistible, I pretend that I haven't noticed him. I pull out a book and try my hardest to look engrossed in what I'm reading; it has to be something cool, yet intelligent . . . let's say *Anna Karenina.* He sees I'm reading an English version and uses this as a pretext to strike up a conversation in his near-perfect yet perfectly adorably accented English. We fall into a deep debate about the Tolstoy masterpiece. He is so enthralled by our discussion that he forgets to get off at his stop. By then he is so enraptured by . . . *me* . . . that he suggests going for coffee, and, unable to leave each other afterwards, we end up going to see an independent artsy movie, which carries over into a fabulous dinner at a romantic bistro, offering up plenty of tasty vegetarian delicacies (no fish!), and of course delicious *vin*, which flows organically into a wonderful and passionate summer *aventure*.

Alas, fate had yet to produce such a dreamy encounter. On the *métro* I've been "asked for the time" on countless occasions (the absolute worst "strike up a conversation" pretext); asked the direction to the next station; just plain accosted and have on occasion bumped into a few people I actually know. Which brings us to my run-in with Jake . . . could something come from this chance encounter?

Jake was a charming, rather successful writer whom I'd known for several years. We were *kind of* friends, in that just-beyond-acquaintances sort of way. I'd never really considered him with any romantic interest, mainly because he wasn't on the market: Jake was in a serious relationship with kids (who were around ten years-old, and so not as bad as Jean-Claude's who were almost as old as me!). He was also about 40, slightly older than my normal dating age limit, though a much more acceptable age than my previous suitor.

When we'd run into each other, I was hurrying through the maze of the Bastille *métro* station, late to meet Pussycat for a concert. Jake was headed in the opposite direction with his *enfants*. We shared a flighty hi-bye kiss on the cheek, and off I went to "storm the Bastille," not quite as triumphantly as the revolutionaries had done 200 years prior, but in an admirably festive way nonetheless.

Admittedly, I may be a bit naïve at times, but I'm not stupid. I received Jake's email (see above) a mere two days after our haphazard run-in. The speed of its arrival was exceptionally quick and the tone awfully friendly, immediately leading me to deduct that he hadn't contacted me just to say "Hello." And lo and behold, in the following emails he revealed that he'd recently separated from his partner and was now living on his own. How convenient. Over the years, Jake and I had exchanged the odd email but nothing on a regular basis. Now he had suddenly taken to writing me every day, and with increasing interest. Soon the casual messages turned into an invitation.

FROM: JAKE   Monday, 5 June 2006 5:22 PM

Maybe we can meet up for a tea, a Molson, or a maple leaf wine sometime.

Sly . . . my suspicions about his true intentions were growing. I had to accept—if only to satisfy my curiosity. Either way, I genuinely liked Jake; he was an intelligent, funny man, and spending time with him was a pleasure. A little *apéro* couldn't really hurt, could it?

FROM: JAKE   Wednesday, 14 June 2006 6:31 PM

Why don't we meet down here at eight? At a café called Le London Calling on the rue Butte aux Cailles? Look forward to seeing you tomorrow.

Our *apéro* date was set. But what should I wear? I wanted to look nice, but not too sexy; after all, we were just meeting up "as friends." I opted for a short-sleeve, button-up black shiny top (with the top two buttons undone) and a knee-revealing, black floral skirt. A dab of perfume later, I jetted on the *métro* going across town.

The Butte aux Cailles was a small cluster of pedestrian streets in the southeast 13th district. Though village-like visually, it was hardly a sleepy place: its growing number of cool bars had turned the area into the "trendy place" to go out for drinks in this part of the city. *Le London Calling* was overflowing with other like-minded *apéro*-goers, so we opted for a less busy bar/restaurant nearby, with a table available on the terrace. Jake charmingly proposed starting with some champagne—a man after my own heart. Our catching-up conversation was so riveting we ordered another glass of bubbly, which eventually led to the suggestion of dinner. *Pourquoi pas?* We hadn't seen each other in a while and had a lot of catching up to do, and we hadn't even gotten around to talking about his latest book project . . . Therefore, it only made sense to pursue our riveting conversation at one of the other hip bars in the area. After he'd paid the dinner bill (bonus points for being a gentleman), we went off to a lively place serving Caribbean punch. It was a bit noisy, and after straining to chat over the chatter and potent punch, he made another proposition.

"I've got a little bottle of champagne chilling back at my place. Care to come up?"

Here we go again! This is when I should have concocted some story about having to get back to Montmartre ASAP to feed my neighbor's cat, or because I had forgotten to turn off my stove (or something like that). However, my story-making skills and common sense had both been compromised by the preceding glasses of champagne, or maybe the punch, or perhaps the offer of more champagne and so I conceded to his offer. A tiny alarm bell rang in my head: *Hey there! What*

are you doing? Is this such a good idea? I just hit snooze. I was a
big girl, I could take care of myself, and Jake was a serious
and respectful man. He would behave. It was just another
glass of champagne . . .

But one thing I always happen to forget is that men are
indeed MEN. They are governed by different logic and
powers than women, and my country naivety was about to
get the better of me . . . or almost.

Upstairs, I was given a little tour of his new abode,
followed by a little verbal tour of his new book. Sneak
previews are always fun (well, depending on what they are of.
Auberge love den rooms—definitely *not* fun!). But shortly after
we had settled down on the sofa with our champagne,
he launched his surprise attack. That's really what it was like;
suddenly I was being suffocated by ferocious, passionate
kisses. Managing to come up for air—and a sip of
champagne—he was moving forward faster than a French
high-speed train! He obviously had intentions of upgrading
this ticket to an over-night *couchette* sleeping car. But I put on
the brakes; I was staying on the slow train.

"I'm conducting an experiment," I joked, taking a big chug
of champagne, attempting to finish my glass.

"What sort of experiment?" enquired Jake, leaning in
closer for the kill, aiming for those shirt buttons.

"It's the first date test," I elaborated, pushing him back.
"I'm trying to see if guys really do call back if you don't
stay over."

In a way, this was a sort of challenge for both of us.
Regardless, I was also not entirely sure I wanted to stay
overnight, or even go out with Jake, if his immediate
intention was just to get me into bed. I wanted a little bit of

romance, not just a one-night stand.

With no real words or moves to convince me to stay, Jake respected my decision and continued to be a gentleman, even paying for my taxi-ride home.

I was very proud of my firmness and my escape. I was sick of the disappearing men act, men who got distracted and "forgot" they had girlfriends, or men who wanted to tick "sleep with a hot blonde" off their lists of 101-things-to-do-before-they-died. *Ha!* We would see if he would reschedule his Lily trip, and perhaps get a long-term rail pass? I suppose I hadn't left his mind, as he sent me a text message a few minutes after I'd gone.

JAKE [06/16/06 12:39 AM]

Maybe u r the angel & I'm the (d)evil
man? Safe return. c u soon. x

Given our mutual wittiness, we'd invented a few new words.

JAKE [06/16/06 12:39 AM]

Eviling, I like the new word.
Eviling itself s great too,
as is naughtification. x

Would I *really* be seeing him soon? He had his kids the following week, but he hadn't forgotten about me.

JAKE [06/16/06 5:49 PM]

Hi Lily, howz about an apero on
Wednesday, say 7PM? c u

Apéro ended up being swapped for lunch. Lunch would do just fine and was maybe even better, or at least less dangerous, than *apéro*. I was interested to see how my experiment would pan out. However, during this little break I hadn't merely been waiting around for him, either. We weren't "officially" dating, and I wasn't even sure if he fit the bill for who I was looking for. On the Saturday night before seeing him again, I'd gone out dancing with the girls and *ran into* an absolutely dreamy Greek God/French Rock Star-type: tallish in stature, dark wavy hair down to his ears (slightly messy), piercing stare, secretive smile, similar to my *métro* fantasy guy—or maybe even better! Here we were, not on the subway car, but rather on the hot dance floor. We eyed each other less and less discreetly. The space between us diminished and soon he was dancing all sexy and close to me; from there, it didn't take long for him to kiss me. He was completely *divine*; however, as divine appearances can be brief, so was the case of my *petit dieu*. All of sudden, he said he had to leave despite (or maybe because of) my pleas for him to stay. Had the girls not been there as witnesses, I would have almost thought he was a figment of my overly creative imagination. I was left saddened and a bit bewildered; he would have made the PERFECT summer *aventure* (well, he was obviously susceptible to disappearing acts, so maybe not, alas!).

Back to my lunch with Jake . . . we met up in another dreamy setting: the Place des Vosges, one of the most beautiful and certainly most romantic squares in Paris. We chose a table on the sunny terrace. Despite the glorious weather, I noted that the mood over lunch was a bit overcast and awkward, even though I did my best to pretend that everything was completely normal between us since our little evening out.

As the waitress set down our after-lunch espressos, Jake sputtered out the reason for his odd behavior. It turned out that after things had ended with his ex-girlfriend/common-law wife a few months ago, he'd started dating another woman, and he wasn't sure where things stood with her. He said he was confused and that he wasn't really ready to start something new just yet . . . I guessed that I was included in this vague scenario of not starting something new along with this other woman. *Hmmpf*—that figures! I did well to have conducted my experiment and not given into him the other night! It seemed that I was now being dumped even before anything had properly started!

In an attempt to keep things light, and to not look like the loser in all of this, I told him about what had happened to a "friend" (the third person works better in some stories like these) over the weekend with the disappearing Greek God/Rock Star.

"Why do men do this sort of thing? They have a beautiful girl in front of them, with all the possibilities in the world, and then they run away."

"Maybe he had a girlfriend? Or perhaps he was suddenly possessed by some Aztec gods?" This was the Jake I liked: clever and funny. Jokes aside, he then revealed a truth about men.

"It's like we are driving along a road, this road being a relationship, and something or other *someone* grabs our attention and we abruptly veer off that road. It's almost like an uncontrollable power overcomes us. Off the road we swerve. Then, as fast as this force might have initially embodied us, we wake up and steer ourselves back onto the 'right road.'"

While this reasoning would seem unacceptable to women, there is some strange logic to it that can explain the (often) peculiar actions of men (still quite inexcusable!). Do they really need blinders to stay on the "right road"? So had both the Greek God/Rock Star sex bomb and Jake acted on the same carnal impulses? I would never comprehend them. We left each other after lunch with the unspoken understanding that if he were to pursue anything with anyone, it would likely be with this other woman. So be it.

Jake was now out of the picture, but I didn't have much time to brood, because it was just at that moment that Foxy cruised onto the scene—leading to the exciting, but oh-too-short, two weeks we spent together. Jake was easily forgotten, at least for the moment, until this message appeared in my inbox:

FROM: JAKE   Saturday, 2 September 2006 9:15 PM

Settling back in, rentréeing . . . Care to get together, during the week maybe?

La Rentrée. The French really get their year started off in September, as many other foreign commentators have noted. This particular time of year is called *La Rentrée* (meaning, "the return") because it is not only back to school time: for most French employees, it's also the time to go back to work after a month or so of holidays. Was Jake trying to get some new things going for his *Rentrée*? Why did he want to see me?

Meeting up would be the only way to find out.

In fact, Jake hadn't totally dropped off the face of my earth over the summer, just on the romantic front. We'd exchanged a few emails, although he hadn't attempted to see me. He'd spent much of the summer traveling and doing research for his upcoming book. I myself had also gone home for a few weeks. Before leaving we'd made a few jokes about Canadian specialties (or rather the lack thereof), and so I thought I'd bring him back a silly little present from my homeland.

FROM: JAKE   Tuesday, 5 September 2006 11:30 AM

Thanks for last night. It was good to spend an evening up on the mountain away from the hustle and bustle of city life, and have a relaxing chat with you. We must do it again sometime. I've found a really authentic Chinese restaurant down here - no, they don't cook badgers, they just have all these Dallas-hairdo Chinese ladies swanning about, and great noodles (available without animal sauces). Thanks also for the present.

Our meeting up in Montmartre was rather innocent. I took him to a cool bar near my place (close, but not *too* close!). Almost like nothing had ever happened, we gabbed on about all kinds of topics: his trip, the weather, nonsense . . . and being the witty guy he was, he was really fond of his present ("moose droppings", well, chocolate covered peanuts in humorous packaging). He suddenly seemed quite keen on seeing me very soon. Was it my gift that piqued his interest again? My fun-loving charm? Or was it the warm, late-summer evening air?

FROM: JAKE   Friday, 8 September 2006 5:45 PM

How about next Friday night for a Chinese feast?
See you next week?

There it was: a new, and real, date. He was indeed quite clever in setting it up as an innocent "meet-up" near my place and then a less-than-innocent one close to his . . .

Jake's apartment wasn't far from Chinatown—well, that's what the area was often called. But, it had no really specific personality or distinctive neighborhood feel like most of the other "Chinatowns" in western cities. There was no Chinese dragon gate beckoning in visitors, or red lanterns decorating the streets; it was merely a bunch of Asian grocery stores and charmless, neon-lit restaurants peppered on the ground floors of ugly 1960s high-rise towers. That didn't mean the food didn't hold promise, or that you wouldn't run into a fun character . . . after all, I was about to discover this "very authentic" Chinese restaurant with its Dallas-esque waitresses.

The restaurant Jake took me to did serve up some good noodles, but the Dallas-esque waitresses weren't "swanning" around. The conversation was light: Jake entertained me with a few good stories from his new book and also shared some aspects about his life as a writer. The evening was flying by and when the check came, it was quickly followed by an: "I've got a bottle of champagne chilling back at home" invitation.

Of course, my naivety had dissolved after the last time I'd heard that line, but what did he really want from me? Did he merely want to beat my experiment? He truly seemed more serious than before. I suppose I was also intrigued and in admiration of Jake. I'd never dated anyone who was somewhat famous, which made the prospects that much more exciting. I was ready to give this a try, and hoped that a little autumn romance would actually lead to something more than seasonal this time around.

So I went back to his place and champagne turned into a *petit déjeuner* of organic English breakfast tea and butter-free croissants . . . I would have to wait to see how the experiment would pan out.

At first it seemed like everything was going well. We were calling and writing to each other often and made plans to see each other when he had free time. I tried not to be bothered by the length of time between our rendezvousing; I knew he was busy and had his family obligations.

His schedule finally had some room about two weeks later. Jake suggested meeting for some drinks in a central location, so we met not far from Châtelet/Les Halles, the city's busiest interchange *métro* station (where I'd run into Julio and his guitar—sniff!), thus convenient for both of us to get to.

I gave him two copies of the little booklets I'd written, hot off the press (and to be launched in an upcoming story). But just like our lunch in Place des Vosges, Jake was acting a bit odd. He was trying to maintain a normal demeanor, but I could see through his bluff. Our pre-meet conversations had been fine, and that night I was being my oh-so-charming self, so I didn't really understand what the problem could be. The time was approaching for the *métro* to close, yet he was lingering, avoiding something.

Finally, he said he was wiped after a busy week and needed to go home. Go home . . . alone? This was very, very suspicious. Was he really tired? Just old? Something was definitely wrong. So off we went on our separate ways.

I was slightly disappointed with this delay, although not heartbroken. He left saying he wanted to see me soon.

FROM: JAKE   Tuesday, 3 October 2006 09:16 AM

It was good to meet up the other evening. Sorry I'm just so utterly knackered. See you soon.

Or so he claimed. But was he telling the truth? When was *soon*? If he really wanted to see me, you would think he could try to make some time. After another week passed without a message, I was starting to get a little antsy. My hopes that I'd achieved my quest for a summer romance (and perhaps was succeeding in securing something more serious) were dismally fading, much like the chances of catching the *métro* at 2:00 am on a Saturday night.

FOXY [10/08/06 7:25 PM]

Hey, my Tigresse!! I'm back from
Manchester! It was amazing!
Off to Australia next week!
I wanna see you before I go!

Ahhhh . . . it would be great to see little Foxy and hear about his Manchester adventures. His liveliness was so tremendously contagious. We met up at a fun little bar outside the *métro* Bonnes Nouvelles—or, the "Good News" station (maybe it could help bring me good news? That Foxy had possibly canceled his trip to Australia?).

We chatted and laughed for hours. Not surprisingly, he started putting on the moves when it came time to leave the bar. However, I wasn't going to misbehave. I told him that I was seeing someone else and thus would be going home alone. I did let Foxy give me a *terribli foxy* kiss good-night, and we parted ways on the *métro* platform. I was very proud of my firm resolve. I could resist temptation and be faithful. But did I have someone to be faithful to? I was less and less sure . . .

The weeks were creeping by without much news from Jake, heightening my concern about "us," when he finally sent word:

FROM: JAKE   Monday, 16 October 2006 9:09:38 PM

. . . also I must admit that I've been trying to get things back together with a girlfriend. I don't want to mess you about, so I thought I'd better let you know. Well, I suppose I have messed you about, but not deliberately.

What! Getting back together with **a** girlfriend? My experiment had been a total failure! I almost couldn't believe it!

"He did what?" exclaimed Naughty, slamming down her glass of wine on the table.

"It seems like he's ditched me for his ex-girlfriend," I moaned.

"You mean his ex-wife?" questioned Special Kay, totally confused over the story.

"No, not his ex-wife, his ex-girlfriend . . . the one after his ex-wife/partner/mother of his children, or at least I think she's from *after*," I mumbled into my quickly emptying glass of wine.

"You don't want to date someone with kids and graying hair anyway," rationalized Pussycat, finishing off hers.

"Yeah, you have a point, but I've been ditched . . . *again!*" And with that I downed my glass of *Saint* (dis)*Amour*.

Pussycat went to refill my liquid heartache medicine, but the bottle was empty.

"Champagne anyone?" she suggested. "We can't let Jake give it a bad name!"

I really didn't understand. Had Jake simply been using me as his own pick-me-up after splitting with his long-term partner? What did this woman have that I didn't? I was pretty sure she was closer to his age, but was that the real deciding factor? I'd never really known his motives. I'd fallen once again for the wily guiles of men, and I was beginning to feel that I would always be merely an object of desire!

The summer had waned and the golden leaves were revealing autumn. I really needed to reconsider my plans for a summer romance . . . a plan that I had failed horribly at . . . *twice*. It was a terrible tennis match between *je t'aime* and *je ne t'aime pas!* Maybe it was time to give up completely, take a break, and really wait for someone who was more definitely looking for something concrete? That sounded like a good, sensible idea—but wait a second, I'd just been kind of dumped! What a shot at my ego . . . *encore!* Maybe I would need another morale booster to get me back on the right track to find someone for a real relationship?

All I knew for sure right now was that I felt desperately lost in the entangled *métro* map of my love life.

❤

VALENTINO [10/18/07 7:18 PM]
Hi there Mademoiselle, how are you?
Just wanted to know how things
were going with you. xoxo

DAVE [10/20/06 7:22 PM]
Care to meet at the usual?

"You might actually have a point there. He was a tad bit deceiving."

"Just a *tad?* Sticking up for your counterpart now?"

"Okay, how about 'quite deceiving'? But I also don't blame him for trying."

"Do men ever think about the consequences of their actions?" I asked venomously.

"I would imagine that some do, but I guess when we are taking in the moment, we can veer off the tracks, or road, or whatever analogy he used."

What would I ever do with men? It seemed they were all runaway trains. I let out a long exasperated sigh and finished off my drink.

"Well, it's a shame men can't act more responsibly . . . or at least be more honest. The amount of times I've run into 'forgetful' men over the past year or so is alarmingly high."

"It seems you have perhaps bewitched them under your charm, making them practically helpless, they just didn't know what to do!" Dave declared.

"It's all *my* fault then. I didn't do anything!"

"Oh, but you don't have to actually *do* anything, it seems to happen naturally."

"To tell you the truth, I'm getting a little fed up with all this."

"You want someone reliable, caring and fun?" He insinuated with a flirtatious smile. I didn't think it was wise to even answer his leading question. I certainly needed a way to forget about my current woes and lamenting to Dave was not proving to be the most beneficial means of doing so.

Summer Romance Resolutions - October

- **Important!** Review past resolution lists—especially the following points:

    - stay away from anyone in or ending a relationship (wife, girlfriend, common-law partner – any!)

    - don't go back to his place on the first date—and also apply if dinner invitation is in nearby restaurant and especially when there is an offer of **CHAMPAGNE**

- Try to figure out if potential candidate has a secret stock of champagne at home on reserve to seduce women

- Be very wary of métro run-ins – more dangerous than I had previously envisioned!

- Avoid men who might have "run off the track" tendencies – this will be a hard one to spot!

- Stay away from anyone WITH children:

    - over 20 years old

    - under 20 years old

    - . . . ANY!

COOKIES AND SHOTS

ARIEL/OREO? [10/22/06 3:32 PM]
*—Salut Lily, it's Ar . . . Great meeting you last night,
I'm calling as promised . . .—*

The summer was officially over and my renewed search for a "summer" fling was already out the window. After being deserted for Australia, sought after by a man almost twice my age, and brushed off by another who actually preferred older women, I was left a little dazed and confused. In this bewildered mental state, the idea of going out to *O'Hooligan's* didn't seem so bad. After all, it was only a Friday night . . . how much trouble could we get into?

The girls came over to my place for a warm-up *apéro* and munchies before we headed down the hill. Fridays were usually less busy than Saturdays; there were just enough people to make the place feel full without being over-crowded. Out on the dance floor, I started exchanging furtive glances with a dark-haired cutie surrounded by a group of friends. He wasn't as drop-dead gorgeous as the French Greek God/Rock Star from the previous story, but not shabby at all.

"Hey Naughty, what do you think of that guy over there?"

"Which one?"

"The cute one," I replied—*wasn't it totally obvious?* Then again, Naughty and I had very different tastes in men; there were no hat-wearing rapper types in sight!

"Looks like he's with that girl," she astutely noted.

"Yeah, but he's been making eyes at *me* since we got here." It was true that he was being a little extra friendly with a certain girl in his group, but it didn't really seem like they were together . . . maybe only a friend or cousin?

We carried on with our little game of cat-and-mouse eye-tag when, suddenly, he made a more daring gesture, meaning something like, "Hey there, come follow me off the dance floor." For a split second I wondered, *Should I stay or should I go?* I should go. But, it was a second too late; by the time I turned around to make my move, a huge wave of people came streaming onto the dance floor, and when I'd finally managed to desperately push my way through it, he was nowhere to be found. I stood there, looking around in a panic, but there was no sign of him. He'd vanished into thin air! I did a little stroll around, scoped out the bar area, but alas, my search was futile. I had no choice but to return to my friends, distraught.

"Oh my God! He's been carried off by a herd of elephants!" proclaimed Naughty, having witnessed what had happened, and now seeing me return miserable and alone.

She was right. All those people who'd madly rushed onto the dance floor *had* seemed like a herd of elephants. I couldn't just let a bunch of party "animals" foil my plans! I would have to put on my safari hat and return to the hunt; after all, I had a rare French lion to catch.

Determined, I pushed my way past the elephants to the edge of the dance floor where, happily, I spotted him standing alone, perhaps waiting for me? I aimed my love rifle and crept up to my prey and fired! Bull's Eye! I'd shot down my target, so now all I had to do was haul him in. It seemed like an easy enough task, but after a brief introduction he blurted out a sort of ultimatum:

"Listen, I'm here with my friends and there's this one girl who likes me and we might hook up tonight. I wasn't sure if I was really into her and then I saw you. I think you're cute so I'm giving you a try before making my decision."

Giving me a try? What was this—a test drive? But instead of calling him a jerk and walking away, I actually stayed and tried talking to him. I didn't want to lose my hard-tracked prize! The music blaring over us, we attempted to get to know each other. I managed to learn that he was studying film (appealing to my artsy tendencies), but it was virtually impossible to talk with Britney Spears bellowing into our ears.

"Well, I'm going back to my friends," he said impatiently.

And with that, he took off, disappearing just as quickly as the first time. *Talk about je ne t'aime pas!* I'd been defeated by the loud lyrics of "Toxic." I was now even more bewildered and distraught. But the more I thought about it, the more I realized that he was the perfect image of a French guy— or perhaps ANY guy. Afraid of commitment, they try to hold onto the hope of someone better coming along, as long as they can. *Hmmpf!* The two of them are probably married now . . . and he's no doubt already cheating on her!

I needed a quick remedy for this new blow, so off I went to the bar for a pick-me-up drink. I squeezed into an empty spot along the counter and waited for the bartender to finish preparing the cocktail he was working on, while trying to decide what I should order . . . something fun, and, more importantly, strong. I must have caught his eye, because before I knew it, he looked up at me, smiled broadly and mimed, "Do you want a shot?" (with his soda dispenser). *Pourquoi pas?* I leaned over the bar and he squirted some soda into my mouth. It started as just a little splash, yet the initial act must have ignited his trigger finger and I was suddenly covered in a mist of Sprite. As I tried to come out of my stunned and "Sprited" state, he grabbed me from the other side of the bar and kissed me—smack dab on the lips! That's what I call forward!

"You could at least give me a real shot for all that!" I huffed when he pulled away. It ought to be a win-win situation. One shot for him, one for me. How could he refuse that after Spriting me? And so, I was served up something like a "sex on the beach" or a "screaming organism."

"Come back before you go, and give me your number."

Well, well, well! That was a lot easier than Mr. Herd of Elephants. I didn't have to prove myself or convince this guy of my worth. The battle of the evening wasn't over. <u>Score</u>: Men 1 – Lily 1. Already forgetting about the first defeat of the night, I went back to dance with the girls. I obeyed the bartender's commands and, before leaving, passed by to give him my number, and he promised to call me the next day. Well, maybe I could give this bartender a shot? It could be nice having a friend who worked at a bar: free cover, free drinks . . . Who needed Jake? Who needed the silly film student? Bring on some *je t'aime*-ing! There was one slight glitch . . . I didn't quite get his name, but, I wasn't too concerned, I figured I'd have it when he called.

The next day I was coming out of the *métro* after doing some therapeutic shopping, when my phone started ringing, alerting me to a new voice message.

—*Salut Lily, it's Ar . . . Great meeting you last night,
I'm calling as promised . . .*—

Awwhh, that was sweet; he hadn't forgotten about me . . . But listening to the message over and over again, I still couldn't figure out what the heck his name was. This would take some sound investigative work, so I called on the help of my favorite detectives over drinks that night.

"It sounds like Oreo," suggested Naughty, after listening to the message a few times.

"It can't be Oreo!" rebutted Special Kay. "That's a ridiculous name. Besides, I'm sure it's copyrighted by Kraft."

"He was wearing a cap so I am not entirely certain, but he could be foreign and have a different sort of name?" I hypothesized. We eventually compromised on Ariel, which was both a girl's and guy's name in France; from the message it definitely sounded like it started with an A.

"Go ahead! Give him a call," dared Pussycat.

"But what do I call him: hey . . . *you?*"

"It's a start. Maybe you'll get his machine and it'll say his name," suggested Naughty.

"Well, here goes," I said fatefully, hitting the redial button.

"*Âllo?*" Darn, he actually answered.

"Hey . . . *you*, it's Lily from last night. I got your message."

After some friendly small-talk, he proposed getting together the next night, a Sunday, as he wasn't working. *Parfait!* Again, this seemed so easy, especially compared to arrogant Mr. "Herd of Elephants."

So, the next day at about five in the afternoon, I found myself on the *métro* heading east to the not-so-nice 19th district (just south of Spanish Bobbie's ghetto neck of the woods). He suggested meeting on the corner outside the station, in front of a dreaded *McDo* golden arches (I hoped he wasn't planning on going there!). The trendy Canal de l'Ourcq was right there; maybe we could go to one of its cool bars?

As I crossed the street towards the *McDo*, I saw a bunch of guys loitering about. It had been dark in *O'Hooligan's*; would I even be able to recognize him? At least he was wearing the same cap, allowing me to pick him out. Getting closer, I couldn't help but notice that he was fairly short, barely taller than me. I hadn't realized that on Friday night, but then again, he had been behind the bar. I shouldn't rule him out just on height (I told myself).

"Hey . . . *you*," I greeted him.

I shouldn't have been surprised when he dove straight in for a kiss after barely saying "Bonjour." This should have been the first cautionary sign. Well, actually, those signs should really have showed themselves the other night in the bar! *What was I doing?*

"I need to stop by *O'Hooligan's*, but then we can get a drink over there if you want?" Well, it was completely in the direction from which I had just come, but never mind.

The *métro* was a bit crowded, so we had to stand. He didn't really have much to say, but he held me close to him and kept trying to kiss me. I attempted conversation, in vain.

This line of behavior continued into the bar. I think he said he was studying economics or something like that, but tearing information out of him was as difficult as tracking that rare lion. I did manage to find out that he was from Morocco. I didn't mind going out with a North African as long as they weren't *über*-religious; my paganism would definitely not go over well in that case. I doubted that he was very religious, if at all, what with his picking up random girls and downing pints of beer. Whenever I would try to get back to a real conversation point, he would quickly put an end to my words with stifling kisses. I realized that this guy was absolutely not serious. *Thanks, herd of elephants!* This wasn't exactly the kind of catch I was looking for. I wanted a bit of a pick-me-up after the disappointing Jake incident, but not to be blatantly *picked up*.

A buddy of his came by to talk to us for a while, after which "Oreo" suggested we leave. This, of course, would have been the ideal moment to offer to take me out for dinner. But he wasn't very hungry. Pasta or anything *at his place* would do. *What? Yeah right, some pasta . . . served up with Lily sauce!*

"Can't we just talk a little more? I barely know you," I meekly requested.

"But we have been talking . . . all this time," he answered. "We know all about each other now."

Yeah, sure we do. I knew that he wanted Lily for dinner and that was all. This wasn't really worth my time. I had to get out of this nasty situation before I was served up sizzling on a plate.

I blurted out some sort of excuse like, "This isn't really what I need right now," or, "I have work to do," or, "since we can't even talk, I had better go." He told me that I would have to figure things out and that I had to call him if I wanted to see him again—not very gallant at all! This whole quest for a fling or a pick-me-up was taking its toll on me and I was about to give up. "Oreo" was certainly not going to help me with my cause.

Woe was really me!

I didn't call him back that week, and didn't hear from him, either. When the weekend rolled around again, our little girl clan converged at Naughty's for some wine and fun, with full evening plans yet to be decided. We'd even managed to wrangle our good friend Lieutenant Steve to join us; he loved having fun, but with a new baby at home, he didn't get the chance to go out much any more.

To make the most of his night out, Lieutenant Steve wanted to go dancing, and so someone suggested going back to *O'Hooligan's*. Somehow that seemed like a good idea; I guess it was after many bottles of wine . . . and after my bold declaration that I could get us all in for free. After all, now that I knew a staff member, that should do the trick.

"But you still don't even know his name," reminded Pussycat, always the rational one.

"Oh, just say you know Oreo," Naughty said, confident of my "getting us in for free" abilities.

"But it can't be Oreo! I'll say I know Ariel; that name makes the most sense."

So down the hill we all went, and then straight to the front of the line to do some negotiating with the doorman.

"Hi there! We're five pretty girls, and we're friends with Ariel," I boldly declared.

"*Ariel?* Who's that?" asked the bouncer.

"You know, Ariel . . . the bartender . . . from Morocco," I replied, trying to keep up the act.

"Oh, you mean *Adil*," he said, finally realizing to whom

I was referring. Giving us the once over, he let all the girls in for free, leaving our lone man, poor Lieutenant Steve, to pay cover charge (yes, there are *some* perks to being a girl).

Well, at least I'd found out his name, but boy, I certainly didn't want to run into him . . . nor another herd of elephants. He was both extremes of *je t'aime* and *je ne t'aime pas*. I was about ready to give up on having any little romantic adventure, to let sleeping *elephants* lie . . . or least lay dormant until next spring, perhaps?

FROM: JULIEN   Saturday, 4 November 2006 5:28 PM

Hi La Tigresse,
I'm very impressed by your email invitation! Wow, I didn't know that you had literary talent. I'm in Seville, I'm sorry for not being able to see you before leaving, my departure was earlier than expected.

DAVE [11/05/06 7:22 PM]
Are you sure don't want to meet up?
I'm so craving to see you!!

I needed to stay away from bars for a while—see resolutions

<u>Post-Summer (??) Romance Resolutions</u>
<u>- November</u>

- This is getting a little silly—STAY AWAY FROM BAR-BOYS! And perhaps bars in general!

- ~~Don't give out phone number — but don't forget to~~ **~~get~~** ~~phone numbers:~~

- Be much more selective about even giving out your number!

- Be wary of random kissers—it really and truly only leads to trouble

- On a similar note: if guy kisses you before saying hi— warning bells should also go off

- Don't become feeble after a little bruised ego . . . and then succumb to bad dating options

- ASK candidate his name and, if necessary, how to spell it

- Try to see if he might have a "trigger finger" and inclinations towards "Sprite-ing"

- If you see elephants, run in the other direction

CHEZ FRANÇOIS

*—Hey Lily, I got your message, I'm really busy,
but why don't you stop by sometime—*

Feather boas and champagne are a tremendously fun,
yet dangerous combination. But when celebration calls . . .

It was official. I was going to become a published writer.
I was soon going to be found on the shelves of some French
bookstores, and my work referenced by the great powerhouse
of modern book-selling: Amazon.com, a truly great
accomplishment for any aspiring scribe. Well, I have to say,
I would never have imagined that my first publication would
be what it was. A critically-acclaimed novel it was not.
Nevertheless, it was still exciting; a first publication is still
a publication.

Back when I was about 12 and in French school, we had
to take "English Class," and as a straight-A student I was
mortified when I'd barely passed an English spelling test.

I also remember pondering for a good while over how to spell *was* . . . a good indication that it *was* time to get out of French school! That *was* for sure. However, the damage had been done: even after returning to regular classes in English, I continued to struggle with my grammar. Thankfully, home computers and word-processing led to the invention of spell-check, thereby lessening some of my linguistic woes. Years later, here I was, teaching English grammar, and writing texts in the English language! How was *that* for a miracle?

I'd been commissioned to write some English business expression booklets by the publishing house that—for better or worse—most of our gang had done some sort of work for over the past few years, beginning when Special Kay became the assistant to the director (the father of the evil Frenchie she used to keep going back to). Recently, Kay had found greener pastures—or rather, sloping fields of grapevines—working for a wine company (much to our immense content, our stock of *Saint Amour* was being augmented by Kay's brand). Naughty had now filled Kay's place as the director's assistant (though not her place as his son's occasional girlfriend), and yours truly was periodically employed by him to translate dreadfully boring abstracts and articles for the economic and medical journals he published.

As his devilish son worked as an auditor for a large American multinational, the publishing house director became convinced that there was a market for teaching material geared towards young French business-people, leading to the birth of my little booklets. They were filled with expressions like: "I'm afraid we have to *downsize* the *workforce*," "Have you submitted our *call for tenders* yet?" and Naughty's particular favorite, "His proposal is certainly *food for thought.*" The whole process had been such a long and painful endeavor, with many false starts and delays, that I was more relieved than overjoyed when it went to print.

Even though attending book launches was one of my favorite hobbies (like art openings—both wonderful social events with good company and free wine), I didn't feel that my little project deserved a launch. I wanted to wait and hold a grand, lavish launch when I published a real masterpiece. However, Naughty would have none of that; she took the launch organizing into her own hands. She'd gone to great lengths, sent out a mass of invitations, and even managed to get the publisher to pay for a case of champagne as well as two cases of wine from the company Special Kay now worked for. She secured the event to be held at our cherished literary haunt: the Canadian Bookshop in Paris. This was sort of the headquarters of the Canadian Club, as its director was the owner of the shop. Hidden away in the heart of the Latin Quarter, with its overflowing shelves of English books, it was the perfect cultural connection between Canada and France. I had no choice but to make an appearance after all of Naughty's efforts.

On the scheduled day, I showed up early to prepare for my small, but hopefully adoring public (promises of free champagne always helped augment attendance). But just as the event was due to start, instead of being faced with a flood of fans, the skies opened and I was faced with buckets of rain! Was this a good or bad omen? If fewer people showed up, there would be more champagne for us . . . but also lower sales. In the end, a fair amount of people braved the tempest. There we were, all crowded inside the tiny bookshop, trying not to knock down the towers of books and, just before the official start of the signing and speeches, I was handed a mysterious bag.

"Put it on," ordered the gift-giver. I looked up to find the soaked but smiling face of Lieutenant Steve. *Oh la la!* What could it be? I carefully opened the bag to find an opulent, white feather boa. How fun! It was surprisingly my first boa (and one that would get a lot of use). I obeyed, putting it on immediately. Let *la fête* begin! My remaining regrets about holding the launch were quickly being washed away with the evening storm.

And a successful night it was! My many faithful friends and students bought a whopping 50 guides, which was not bad for a first book launch. I managed to enjoy at least a bottle's-worth of the bubbly on my own while being thoroughly entertained by role-plays from the booklet, exuberantly performed by the girls. All in all, we had a very pleasurable and rather drunken time.

The night's festivities were not to end at the bookshop. After cleaning up and finishing off the last bottles of wine, some of us carried on celebrating this momentous occasion at a trendy new restaurant that we'd been meaning to try: *Chez Nicolas*. I left my boa on for good luck and immediately befriended all the waiters in the restaurant. My bubbly champagne attitude most certainly played a role in my popularity that evening.

What a fabulous night it had been . . . it would be a shame to go home and end it. But alas, the girls had to work the next day, so we headed home (I'd purposefully left my schedule free the next day, having foreseen a potentially debilitating headache). I still had my boa on, and might have been acting just a tad silly (singing while twirling around a support pole).

Oddly enough, the other passengers in our *métro* car didn't find me very funny. Why did Parisians have to be so serious? But for once, I was going to tell—or rather show—them what I thought. As our train was pulling into my station, I whipped out my finger gun and "shot" several of the snottier-looking ones. *Bang! Bang! Bang!* The buzzer sounded and off I jumped, with smoking-gun hands, waving *bonne nuit* to them and the girls. At least that got a smile out of the crabby passengers.

Quite satisfied with my daring *métro* shoot-out, I strolled (not exactly straight) up my old street towards my new one. Nearing the top, I spotted a few guys sitting in front of my old nemesis bar, *Chez François.* Back when I was living across the street, it had been the source of many sleepless nights. The boisterous nocturnal revelers would keep me awake until ungodly hours; then, as soon as I would fall asleep, the early-morning beer deliveries would begin and I would be rudely awoken by the racket of clanking beer kegs. I liked having fun and staying up late, but not *every* night of the week, and not because others were having fun without me! One time, I resorted to the "if you can't beat them, join them," theory and went in for a drink with a friend. Entering the bar, I even had lofty hopes it could possibly become my local hang out, an idea that was quickly squashed by the nasty barmaid who kept ignoring us, and who instead served any local who approached the counter. Apparently, I would never become one of "them" and thus vowed never, ever to return.

However, the management had recently changed hands. As I had to walk in front of it practically every day, the new bartender caught my eye. He was tall and thin with curly, dark hair, wore black retro glasses, and though he wasn't necessarily good-looking, he had a quirky aloofness that appealed to me. He looked like a creative challenge, with intellectual potential.

One night, during the week before my booklet launch, I'd been slowly climbing the hill, plugged into my iPod and possibly singing along, when I looked up to see the barman standing outside chatting with a regular. Our three sets of eyes met, so I courageously greeted them with a *"bonsoir"* as I passed by . . . though my bravery petered out there, I didn't dare actually stop to talk to them. I quickly scurried the rest of the way up the hill, and safely tucked myself into bed . . .

. . . Which brings us back to the fateful night of the book launch. As I neared *Chez François,* I saw the barman sitting outside, having a drink. I don't really remember how it happened (again, it might have been courtesy of the boa), but all of a sudden I was sitting beside him, cocktail in hand. Then, what seemed to be all of a sudden (yet again), I was snuggled up (fully-clothed) on a bench at the back of the darkened bar, covered by a jacket, my head resting on someone's lap . . .

My head was in fact on the lap of François, which turned out to be the name of the bartender. *Oh no,* I was going to be in trouble. The girls had made me pledge against bar boys (especially considering what had happened with the last one! Oh, and I guess all the others before . . .). But did this really count? It wasn't really a bar pick-up, in the traditional sense of meeting *in* a bar. Or was it? Besides, we were just sitting/lying there. I was making goofy conversation in my lingering champagne haze as he gently caressed my messed-up hair, and laughed at my stupid jokes.

Light began creeping in through the back window.

What time was it? *Yikes!* Somehow it was already 10:00 am. We got up and François made us some coffee; I would need more than that to get over this nasty hangover, but for now it was helping me come back to the world of the sober. I could only imagine the physical state I was in: a Parisian savage with a disastrous head of hair and raccoon eyes from smudged mascara. It would be a short, but risky, walk-of-shame home.

Montmartre is like a village in more ways than one, and knowing a handful of local shopkeepers and my neighbors had its pros and its cons. Short as the distance was, could I make it up to my street and sneak inside my building without running into anyone I knew? I tried to fix myself up as much as possible and tucked my boa into my bag; nevertheless, my all-black outfit, right down to the tall black boots, hardly gave me the appearance of someone out for a mid-morning business appointment. Having left my place when it was already dark the evening before, I didn't even have a pair of sunglasses in my bag to hide behind. I bade François farewell and he told me to stop by again soon.

Exiting the bar, I shielded myself from the bright light of day and walked as swiftly as possible the rest of the way up the hill. I made it past my usual bakery without the friendly sales girl spotting me. I flew unnoticed past my next hurdle: the *épicerie*-convenience store with its flirtatious vendors. *Whew*, only two more challenges to overcome: Mr. and Mrs. Grouchy Neighbor. While I enjoyed living in a bigger apartment, it came at a price . . . dealing with complaining crotchety neighbors; one above, and one across from me. Thinking that I was a bit of a party-animal (well, maybe with *some* good reason), I was sure that catching me creeping home at 10:30 am in the middle of the week in what was clearly evening attire would certainly make their days.

I turned onto my street . . . so close! I carefully punched in my door code, rounded the corner into the courtyard and who was standing there, almost as if she was waiting for me? Mrs. Nosey from upstairs, gossiping away with the concierge. I forced out a quick *bonjour* and hurried across the courtyard, a few feathers trailing behind, leaving them with something new to gossip about!

So I now had a bartender/bar proprietor friend. Julio from *The Reindeer* and Adil from *O'Hooligan's* didn't really count, as they were mere employees. François on the other hand actually owned his bar. I was keeping my encounter a little hush-hush with the girls for the time being in order to avoid any preemptive criticism. I wanted to see if anything would come of it first. Nevertheless, I wasn't exactly sure what to make of the somewhat awkward situation with him; it wasn't like he'd taken my number or anything. But then again, nothing had really happened between us either (nothing that I could remember, anyway!). How would I go about seeing him again? Could I just drop by the bar? Would he be happy to see me? Well, no better way to find out than to try.

The following weekend, on my way home at around 1:00 am (this time not in a complete champagne stupor), my eyes fixated on Pierre, the other guy who'd been with François when I'd said *"bonsoir"* a few weeks before; and, I vaguely remembered him being there on the launch night as well. He beckoned me inside, and as François was busy serving drinks, I sat down at the corner of the bar and chatted away with Pierre. The more I got to know him, the more I began to think he might actually be a more appropriate "catch" than François. To start, he was much cuter than François: he always dressed like a dapper English gentleman with a suit jacket and a little cravat, perfectly fitting the *oh so British* English accent he put on. Through our conversation, I learned that he'd studied art history and was now working at a hip art center. Wasn't that more interesting than working at a bar? He also sold antiques in his spare time, upping his artsy coolness. So what was the problem with trying to hook up with Pierre?

François. What about François? Since my memory was a tad blurry about the other night, I wasn't really sure if Pierre was aware of my passing out on François' lap. Was it bad tact to "forget" that I had been snuggling up with François the week before and try to jump ships? Pierre also seemed genuinely interested in me, while François was keeping his remote attitude. However, near the end of the night, another girl showed up who seemed quite attached to Pierre. It was hard to tell if she was his girlfriend or if she just wanted to be. He wasn't exactly reciprocating her extra friendliness, although I couldn't be sure, and wasn't going to play with fire.

Soon the bar was closing up and the shutters pulled over the windows. A few regulars were lingering around for some extra drinks and I was also invited to stay. Was I finally going to attain the "regular" status too?

Over the next few weeks I stopped by periodically, almost always late, and I would stay even later. But not too much ever happened between François and me. He would chat with me between serving customers, and, when everyone left, we would have a few more drinks. The evening would end at a vague time, several hours later, with me falling asleep on his lap after a kiss or two. It was obvious that he was fond of me, but even more obvious that he did not want to get attached to anyone. Pierre often stayed after closing time, too, and as he could see that something was going on between François and me, he kept his distance.

It was now mid-November and certainly too late for a "summer" romance. I was really and truly ready to abandon the project altogether (and was very close to regretting ever having pursued such a quest in the first place!). I knew that I now wanted something more, especially during and after things with Jake. I doubted that I was headed in that direction with François, however much I was trying to convince myself to just wait and see.

One night, as we were hanging out after hours with the regulars, François spontaneously invited me over to his place. He left the bar in the not-so-careful hands of bottomless-glass Pierre (I soon realized why he hung around the bar so much), and off we went on his scooter.

He didn't live too far away, just south of Montmartre near the *Grands Boulevards* area. The heart of 19th-Century *Haussmannian* Paris, its wide boulevards were lined with the typical beige stone buildings of the era, layered with elegant apartments and dotted with historic cafés. It turned out that his parents owned one of these famous *brasseries*. Coming from this family tradition, perhaps François was trying to do his own thing with his little bar, to prove that he could do something on his own and successfully.

François lived around the corner from this café, in a large apartment that used to belong to his grandmother. And it still looked like she lived there, too, the walls and shelves covered with dusty family heirlooms. I doubted that he really spent much time there. I was learning more about the mysterious François. He'd lived in this apartment with his ex-girlfriend for a number of years and still had things of hers around: makeup, creams, clothes . . . These artifacts were a little suspicious; was she really an *ex*-girlfriend? Chances were she was really an *ex*, as there weren't *too* many of her belongings about, and his place still oddly looked like a bachelor pad (or a museum). I asked him why he didn't just throw her things away or give them back, and he said they had sentimental value (I guess like keeping the apartment in the same condition as when his grandmother had lived there?). He was very attached to the past; perhaps that's why he couldn't enjoy the present.

At least on this particular night, we lay down on a real bed and not the uncomfortable bar bench. But we didn't really do much more than we had the other nights back at the bar. He told me I was too beautiful for him and that I shouldn't be with him . . . I should just forget about him. Who was I supposed to be with, then? Was I condemned to wander, and to be forever lonely?

François wasn't a caller; even though he had my number, he only ever called me once. A Saturday or two after our excursion to his place, I stopped by the bar just before closing time. He practically ignored me and was being extra-friendly to a woman I'd seen in there before. And then suddenly he kind of kissed her! I was *not* a happy camper. What was I to think? I left almost straight away, hurt. Okay, he was a bit strange in general and had told me to forget him, but he didn't have to kiss other girls when I was there (it wasn't a huge, passionate kiss, but STILL!). As much as I'd been trying to hide this strange relationship from the girls, the time came for me to ask for some advice.

"He did *what?*" exclaimed a wide-eyed Naughty. "I can't believe it! Maybe she was his ex?"

"Maybe . . . but still, I can't really go on just waiting around for him."

"Absolutely not!" And with that, she helped me concoct a text message to him, something along the lines of: if he wanted to kiss other girls then I wasn't going to come by the bar anymore.

He didn't reply right away, but a few days later he called and left me a message.

—Hey Lily, I got your message. I'm really busy, but why don't you stop by sometime—

He didn't say anything about the slightly evil message I'd sent, but he did add something about being in Normandy and that he'd be back in a few days . . .

As the weeks passed, my interest in dating weird François was waning. Okay, it was true: he was different from my latest failed conquests, but this was obviously going nowhere. I'd gone from someone who only wanted to kiss me to someone who never called and didn't seem to care about me. In not wanting the former, I got its polar opposite!

I avoided stopping by for a week or so; I even began going completely out of my way, taking other streets to get home so I wouldn't have to walk in front of the bar. But then one night, when I did go past, Pierre spotted me and pulled me inside. He was happy to see me, got me a drink and kept me company with witty chatter and jokes. François seemed to be flirting with this new, sort of trashy-looking girl. I didn't really care . . . okay, well maybe just a little . . . but that night I was having much more fun giggling with Pierre. After closing, François gave the keys to Pierre and left along with the tarty girl. *Hmmpf!* Well, that was that. Obviously, he was just looking for a little action. He had this sex-driven, demented look in his eyes. Given his tepid treatment of me, and seeing him leave with Trasherella, I would never understand his logic; there was no way of really knowing who he was at his core. And besides, I was ready to move on and forget about *Chez François*.

I looked over at Pierre. Was there any real potential with him? If not, couldn't I find someone just to spend a little time with? Someone who was interesting, but not too complicated? Someone who would pay me enough attention, be a little *je t'aime*-y and not downright ignore me and *je ne t'aime pas* me? Was that too much to ask for? Or should I just go into winter hibernation instead?

♥

ELIJAH [11/24/2006 05:49 PM]
. . . just remembering a spilly wet bed,
I'll try fixing it tomorrow

DAVE [11/26/06 6:57 PM]
Free tonight? It's cold and rainy,
your spirits could help cheer me up.

"Well, don't despair; there are other fish in the sea."

"I know, I know."

"François probably has a difficult romantic past, that's all. It can sometimes take quite a while to get over a major heartbreak."

"I don't know if that was really the reason behind his behavior. Regardless, it seemed like a dead-end and I never knew what he expected."

"Some men express their feelings in subtle ways; others are more open . . ." Dave's hand was creeping across the table.

"I don't understand men at all!" I declared fervently, while reaching for my glass to thwart his attempted caress.

"I suppose this encounter proved that you can meet someone when you least expect it . . . and close to home . . ." said Dave with a little twinkle in his eye.

"Close to home hasn't brought me very much luck, actually!"

"And I would have been so sad should you have abandoned *Le Rendez-vous* for this other bar."

"Oh Dave, I would never abandon our café." *Uh-oh, that was the wrong thing to say!*

"Maybe we could *rendez-vous* here more often, then. The quality of the clientele is much better than this *Chez François* place, and I'm sure you could find the perfect man right here."

"*Um, ahh*, well, I'll still be coming by, but actually I was thinking that I need to go into hibernation for a little while and, you know, give myself a complete break from men . . . should we get the bill?" I had to get out of this mess before he made an even bigger move.

"You can start your hibernation tomorrow; are you sure you don't want to come back to my place? It would mean so much to me. You're looking absolutely divine."

"No!" I yelped. "*Ummm, ahhh*, I have to work early tomorrow!" And for the rest of my life, or at least on days after drinks at the *Rendez-vous*.

Pre- New Year's Resolutions - 2007

(We're pretty much at the end of the year—plus going into serious HIBERNATION—so might as well get resolution writing over with now)

- See each and every resolution list of 2006 **plus**:
- Stay far, far away from the following:

    - **BAR-BOYS** (boys you meet in bars, bartenders, bar owners - anyone with any connection to a BAR)

    - men with anyone in tow: wife, girlfriend, haunted memory of ex-girlfriend, children, herds of elephants

    - men whose names you don't know

    - men who don't know how to use a phone

    - men who seem like they don't like you (= they probably really don't!)

    - a full head of gray hair

- Be wary of lunch, dinner, day-trip or weekend getaway invitations (well, we could also add breakfast invitations—that didn't make the list last year)

- Don't drudge up anyone from the past

- Make sure candidate is DEFINITELY going to be in Paris!

A SOMEWHAT SUCCESSFUL "FRENCH" INVASION

LAURENT [12/03/06 4:04 PM]
My head is full of images! I so
terribly want to see you tonight!
Who are you seeing tonight?!!

During my years Paris, I'd come to the conclusion that there are two types of Frenchmen:

Type #1 falls in love/lust with you immediately; let's call them the "*je t'aim*-ers." With this type, instant cries of "*Je t'aime!*" are passionately emitted, accompanied by a gazillion text messages a day. They can't live without seeing or talking to you every day, and while in your presence they stick to you like gooey Camembert, constantly oozing with affectionate (cheese-, wine- or tobacco-scented) kisses. This may seem romantic to some, but it can also be completely tiresome to others, myself included.

Type #2 is all aloof (sort of like François); they could be referred to as "*je ne t'aime probably pas*-ers." It's not that they play mind games, but at first you can't really decipher what they really want. Are these guys actually interested in you? Do they *hate* you? They are more of a silent-killer bunch.

Surprisingly, relationships with Type #2 can sometimes succeed in the end, while some of the relationships with Type #1 can conversely end up as a *désastre total*.

I'd just come from a luke-warm version of Type #2. I'd been bemoaning to myself that I wanted a little more of Type #1, but really just a smidgen . . . however, I had to be careful what I wished for. Another round of destiny's twisted game was about to begin, and I knew it would be a dangerous one the very minute I met my new adversary.

It was December 2ⁿᵈ, a Saturday night. 19 days until the official start of winter and, after my recent defeats with the bar boys, I was more than ready to slip into cozy boy-less hibernation. Could I make it safely to the 21ˢᵗ without incident?

Pussycat, Special Kay and I were meeting up with an American/French couple and a few of their friends for dinner at a restaurant in the lively *Oberkampf* area, one of the evening hotspots of Paris. Dinner sounded harmless enough in my pre-hibernation state of mind. Boys were far from my mind . . .

When we arrived, fashionably late as one does in Paris, the rest of the *invités* were already there and seated. A quick tour around the table for hello-kisses and introductions brought me face-to-face (or rather lip-to-cheek) with someone new. Our mutually sparkling green eyes fused with that electrical charge of fate. *Uh-oh!* This could only lead to one thing: trouble (and that I should maybe just stay away from absolutely anyone with green eyes)!

As it happened, I was assigned the empty seat at the head of the table, next to the stranger. His name was Laurent, he seemed to be in his mid-30s, had short dark hair, wonderfully dazzling eyes and a soft, sly smile that counterbalanced his sturdy, athletic build. It turned out that he was from the southwest of France, the heart of French rugby, clearly evident in his muscular stature. Laurent's physique was put to good use in his job as a *gendarme*. France has both policemen and a sort of military police called *gendarmes* (literally "men of arms" . . . *ooh la la!*), and while I can't really explain the difference, I do know that both police groups look fantastic in their tight, sexy uniforms. I snapped out of my racy policemen dream to the reality of his professional declaration . . . *Yikes!* I'd already tried going out with a military man! I doubted he could be as complicated as my jet fighter pilot, but who was I to tell—I was far from a good initial judge of character. Did I also have to be wary of this one?

He stared at me all through dinner and didn't speak to anyone else. I was a helpless and hopeless victim of his gaze with no way of escaping! A few times, I thought I was going to break into a fit of giggles, finding relief from my uneasiness with frequent, large gulps of wine. Amidst all the staring, Laurent did manage to do *some* talking, and he ended up being rather interesting, and interested . . . in learning everything he could about *me*.

The night didn't harmlessly end with dinner. Someone suggested heading down the street to a fun little South American bar for a mojito (from experience, was this such a good idea?). As we got up from our seats at the restaurant, Laurent's ocular stronghold on me was broken. At the mojito bar, I purposefully sat on the other end of the table from him, next to Pussycat. He was getting a little too intense!

"So, Laurent seems really into you!" she noticed with a coy smile.

"Yeah, but he's a . . . *gendarme!* I can't date a cop! Actually, he's even worse—a *traveling gendarme*—so it's not like I would ever get to see him. Even if he were totally one-hundred-percent cool, it would never be able to work."

Besides, I didn't think meeting anyone right now was a good idea anyway. I had made a pledge to hibernate; I didn't think a winter romance was what I needed to warm me up.

Our group laughed and chatted and soon we'd polished off our mojitos. *Oltro mas?* Our festive attitudes and the little devils on our shoulders beckoned us to pursue our Friday night fun at a bigger, livelier bar next door.

This time, Pussycat and I were seated side-by-side, across from Laurent. Our drinks were decorated with colorful glow sticks. One thing led to another, and the glow sticks turned into weapons of mass . . . *seduction!* Adversaries: Laurent, Pussycat and Lily. Goal: position glowing bait in a sexy place to be removed by the male participant, using whatever means necessary—including (or especially) teeth. The game pushed the racy limits . . . but it didn't totally exceed them, either. Nonetheless, it certainly excited participant number one, who probably thought he had a threesome in store!

Even after all those mojitos, I was still lucid enough to gauge the situation. Here we were, the three of us. While Pussycat was egging Laurent on and flirting to the extreme, I knew her and figured she was just playing with him (not that he could see this for what it really was). And, Pussycat was the youngest of our group and there was more than ten-years of age difference between the two of them, so practically

210

speaking, they did not make a good match. Either way, I didn't know if I was really interested in the manly man drooling over us. He was nice, but not really my type. I was hoping for someone a little creative or at least international. He was the complete *opposite* of François and Pierre. However, if I really thought about it, maybe that was what I needed: just a sweet guy to have a little fun with. Maybe the fact that he traveled was actually sort of thrilling, too. We could see each other a few times over the next few months, which would tide me over until spring?

It came time to leave, and joining arms, our *threesome* headed up the street, past the *Bordela Braziliana* (yikes, surely a bad omen!) and towards the night bus stops. It seemed that we were all innocently going our separate ways, and to our respective homes/destinations; Pussycat to the south, me to the north, and Laurent . . . where was he headed?

"I'm staying with some friends near Place de Clichy," he divulged.

Oh dear, the first step down the wrong path. Place de Clichy was very close to my place. Was he just making that up? Had he heard me say where I lived? We were bound to be taking the same bus and there was no way around it. We gave our goodbye kisses to Pussycat and jumped aboard our fated bus.

I tried to make normal conversation in a pathetic attempt to diffuse some of the sexual tension. I didn't think taking him home was such a good idea, not only because I thought we were so wrong for each other (even though he was attractive), but more importantly, because of Pussycat. She did seem sort of into him, even though they didn't seem to be a perfect match either. Nevertheless, men can be awfully persuasive and Laurent must have learned to be exceptionally perseverant in the army:

"It's still pretty early . . ." (*By this time it was about 3:30 am.*)

"We can just have one more drink together . . ." (*After the* **ten** *we'd already had?*)

"We could just have a cup of tea . . ." (*Cognac-infused . . .?*)

"We don't have to do anything . . ." (*That was a famous line . . . yeah right!*)

"I won't stay long . . ." (*The French were bad at keeping track of time, what with always being late or running behind!*)

I wasn't made for war; I'm a pacifistic, peace-loving Canadian after all, and I give in way too easily. Little did I know that this invasion would end up like Napoleon trying to take over Europe . . . Battle after battle, Laurent would win some territory, get pushed back to his borders, and yet launch a new offensive, employ another method of attack and prove to have the greatest level of persistence ever recorded in Lily-tary history!

His first maneuver was relatively successful. He'd convinced me to let him come back to my place, but I made him promise to behave. We would have a cup of tea. *What was I getting myself into?*

We got to talking—over our herbal tea (really)—and in fact, he explained that he wasn't really a policeman at all, but rather a personal trainer within the army. He was also very well-read and into other things besides knowing the best ways to defend the French President. He was gaining some terrain, which increased with his skills at kissing and flattery (*ummmh*, okay, so there were a few kisses after the tea).

He was going to be in Paris for a few days before being sent back to his base in the southwest. As you might recall, the night he stayed over (*ummmh*, okay, I also let him stay over, but nothing *really* happened after the tea and goodnight kisses) was a Saturday and thus it was already Sunday when he left. However, come morning, he didn't want to leave; his insistent behavior from the night before had returned in full force! Even though it was a Sunday, I still had to go to work (which at this point meant grappling with a painful translation project that had been consuming all of my weekends for months). Therefore, I needed him to leave early so I could have my space to work. He was devastatingly sad to have to go and, before leaving, begged to see me later that day. *Non.* What about that night? I was still going to be working . . . so again . . . *NON!* How about the next evening? Struggling, I didn't have a ready-made excuse for the Monday night, so I caved. The next evening would be . . . fine. All I wanted at that very minute was for him to leave! I would have to deal with the consequences later. He left, seeming quite satisfied with his victory.

Whew! I thought I'd gotten rid of him for the time being, so I made myself a good strong cup of boy-less tea and sat down to work in peace. *Did I say 'in peace'?* I soon realized that Laurent had left in person but not *in spirit*—he haunted me the rest of the day with a constant stream of text messages! The first of hundreds to come!

Let's say he left at 9:30 am.

LAURENT [12/03/06 10:01 AM]
Hurrah for tomorrow my dear
Tigresse! Big naughty kisses
. . . have a great day!

So the first message was a little cute . . . back to work I went.

LAURENT [12/03/06 10:57 AM]

Monday, I'll come directly with
my things If you want? If not
I can come later if you prefer?

What's this about . . . things? I didn't know this was going to be some formal coming-over event. What happened to a few drinks and we'll see?

LAURENT [12/03/06 11:00 AM]

Tomorrow can't come fast enough,
can I come back now?

No, no, and *NO!* What was he on, some magic love drug? He needed to calm down!

LAURENT [12/03/06 11:02 AM]

I'm waiting impatiently for your answer!

Mon dieu! Couldn't I just have a little peace? No means no! He really couldn't take a hint. Maybe he was just swept up in a passionate fury, but Laurent was starting to get a little (or a lot) annoying.

LAURENT [12/03/06 11:17 AM]

As you want. Do you want me to
drop off my things tomorrow
morning b4 I go to work?

Jeez, what were these "things" that he kept talking about? Was he planning to move in or what?

LAURENT [12/03/06 11:23 AM]
Ok I'll call you tomorrow
morning, kisses

Fine, we would see the next day. Would he then leave me alone for the rest of the day?

LAURENT [12/03/06 2:13 PM]
How's your work coming along?
I really can't wait to see you . . . kisses

I had a few hours respite, and was hoping to work productively . . . if only Laurent could have upheld this cease-fire . . . no rest for the war-weary!

LAURENT [12/03/06 3:24 PM]
Hi there, how are you Tigresse?
I really, really can't wait to see you,
let's talk about passion . . . kisses

Passion? I was busy translating the economics of the Industrial Revolution; my mind was far from thoughts of passion. I opted to ignore his message. Maybe that would make him get the hint.

LAURENT [12/03/06 4:04 PM]
My head is full of images! I so
terribly want to see you tonight!
Who are you seeing tonight?!!

No! I think I must have made something up about seeing someone else that night. Was he getting jealous already?

LAURENT [12/03/06 4:07 PM]

Have you looked into
next weekend?

Talk about jumping the gun! If he couldn't wait a day to
see me, how could he be thinking about a week from now?
Then I remembered. To make him leave that morning, I'd
said I might come down to the south to visit him the
following weekend. He had a good memory; I barely
remembered making the promise and now going down to see
him really didn't seem like such a great idea.

LAURENT [12/03/06 4:43 PM]

And so??

My goodness, he would certainly earn himself the title of
Mr. Persistent. However, there might not be a prize to go
along with that. *Leave me alone!*

LAURENT [12/03/06 4:44 PM]

Ok, my suitcase is packed!

Suitcase? I finally had to reply to his message so I could
blow him off for the day, although I doubted that would buy
me much peace. Surprisingly, I only received one
more that day:

LAURENT [12/03/06 10:01 PM]

Have a sweet dream! Kiss

I wasn't sure if I would be having "a sweet dream," what
with this imposing dread creeping over my mental battlefield.

It seemed that all was quiet on the Western Front. However, a fresh assault would begin the following evening.

LAURENT [12/04/06 8:25 PM]
I'm in Barbès station!

By the time he reappeared at my place—not soon enough for him, and way too soon for me—I had little, if NO desire to see him. He'd repelled me with his endless barrage of messages and now I was stuck with him in person, which was ten times worse! Luckily for me, he had to leave for the south the next day, so he was only staying one night (hence the suitcase). Otherwise, I feared he would NEVER leave and then hold me captive as his love slave in my own home! He had certainly proven himself worthy of his military rank; he could probably coerce his way into a Russian spy submarine by assailing it with continual Morse code messages!

Somehow I survived the sleepless night (Laurent's persistence and endurance went beyond his text-messaging) and was all too happy to get rid of him early the following morning.

LAURENT [12/05/06 11:46 AM]
Hi my pretty Lily, are you ok?
I miss you! See you soon, big kiss

. . .

LAURENT [12//0606 06:48 AM]
Have a good day my lovely teacher.
I like you a lot!!! Kiss

Message upon message (with or without horrible attempts at English) was sent; some days I got around ten, others closer to 20! I replied to an average of two per day if I felt I absolutely had to. This sort of assault-by-text behavior might make some girls swoon and fall in love, but it was driving me up the wall! I was going from a guy who never called me to one who wouldn't leave me alone for a second. I was wondering how I'd ended up with such romantic extremes! *Jeez*, all I wanted was just a little more attention; this was not a middle ground.

As I've already admitted—and pathetically demonstrated—I'm very bad at getting rid of men, and it seemed like the battle with Laurent would be my biggest challenge yet. Maybe the easiest way to solve the problem was to change my phone number? *Hmmm*, that wouldn't be effective enough: he could eventually track me down right to my doorstep! For the time being, I fabricated some impossible excuse about not being able to go down to visit him the next weekend. Then I was going off to South Africa to visit my fabulously fun sister Cori (who'd moved there after falling for a cute South African), so we wouldn't be able to see each other for about six weeks. With any luck he would just forget about me while I was away. I told him I was leaving my phone behind so there would be no point in trying to contact me. By a stroke of luck, or thanks to the many gods I prayed to for help, he hadn't asked me for my email, so I hoped I'd be safe from his blitz for a few weeks.

Just before leaving, Laurent dropped an odd comment into one of our few phone conversations. Apparently, all this time he'd been sending me messages, he'd also been chatting with Pussycat. I think it was merely in a friendly way, but you never really know . . . What I did know was that he was trying to use this as a sort of psychological bargaining chip in a bid to win me over:

"Oh, I really like you, Lily, but I'm not totally sure . . ."

Not sure of what? What about all those messages? Were they sent with only friendly intentions? Had something been lost in translation? Laurent went on to say that it was good I would be going away for a while because he wanted to "think about things," in order to decide if I was the right person for him. Well, he could think as long as he wanted. I had nothing to think about; I did not want to pursue anything, except the fastest escape-route out of this mess! Nevertheless, I was totally incapable of being up-front. I had to cowardly acknowledge that, up until that point, I still hadn't told him that I wasn't interested in him. I was just biding my time till my trip . . . and dreaming about finding a cute South African boy for myself (it was *summer* down there after all!) . . .

South Africa was indeed the perfect escape! My surrogate Italian sister decided to come along and my real sister Cori ensured that we had a fantastic time—a little more than innocent family fun. After many bottles of delicious regional wine and a flirtatious few days with another tasty, fair-haired local specialty (who was full "bodied," had a sexy palate . . . and in my opinion was an excellent vintage), I had practically forgotten about my love-struck stalker. If only it could have been that easy—six weeks was not enough time for him to forget about me!

__BIENVENUE EN FRANCE__

Welcome to France.

Who was there, greeting passengers disembarking from my plane at Charles de Gaulle airport? *Les Gendarmes.* In addition to the myriad of other tasks the men of arms had, they were also in charge of airport security. I didn't think Laurent was among the airport guards on duty when I arrived, but he wasn't far . . . encountering these men in uniform was a bad omen . . . in fact, I'd received a message from the particular *gendarme* in question, mere hours after I'd landed. The ceasefire was over—he was back on the offensive, launching his Lily-counter-attack.

LAURENT [01/17/07 3:25 PM]

Welcome back pretty Tigresse!
I'm in Fontainebleau,
when can I see you?!

Oh God, what kind of excuse could I make up this time? Maybe it would be better to gather up enough courage, meet him face-to-face, and surrender? No wait, surrendering would mean giving in to him. Maybe we could sign a non-aggression pact instead?

LAURENT [01/17/07 12:10 PM]

Hi, is it always ok for 8:30
in front of the opera? Kiss

I had to build up my courage and tell him. So we set a date to meet for a drink—one drink. Travelling on the *métro* to our meeting point at the Opera Garnier (the meeting point with Dean), my mind was abuzz, busy concocting a believable story as to why I didn't want to see him anymore. Maybe I could say that I'd gotten engaged in South Africa? That I'd found the love of my life? That I was moving there . . . *next week?*

I should have better prepared my defensive line. I was dealing with a professional warrior after all. As soon as he saw me, a huge smile spread over his face. He had enough restraint to only give me a kiss on the cheek—so far so good.

We sat down at a quiet table and I ordered the strongest liquid courage on the menu. As soon as our beverages arrived, and before I could utter a word towards my freedom, Laurent broke into a lengthy and passionate soliloquy about how he'd done some thinking over the holiday about his life, future, and matters of the heart. He was 35 and not getting any younger, so perhaps it was time to settle down. Maybe he was right; he should settle down, but it wasn't going to be with me! He declared that he hadn't been able to stop thinking about me over the "break." He would do anything to be with me. In fact, he said that the town he lived in wasn't that far from Paris—only a three-hour high-speed train ride! We could go back and forth on the weekends and then he would ask for a transfer to Fontainebleau. It was only an hour from Paris, so we could still live there. *What's this WE business all about?*

Without consulting me, he had come to the conclusion that I was the woman for him.

Could I say no to those beautiful words, sparkling green

eyes, and cute little smile? *Oui!* They were not enough to win me over. I just wasn't into him, and all his persistence had totally turned me off. But instead of telling him that and trying to put an end to this painful story, I gutlessly escaped with an "I'll have to think about it" (*would I ever learn?*). However, my usual method of not returning phone calls didn't work with this one; his messages just kept coming.

LAURENT [01/18/07 12:18 PM]

Hi lovely and sexy and hot teacher.
What are you doing Friday afternoon?
I can be in Paris at I PM and leave that
night or the next day. I want you and
our shared pleasures...

Of course, I didn't reply to this message, only to get more later in the day.

LAURENT [01/18/07 8:42 PM]

Is it OK for tomorrow?

I had to stay strong, I wasn't going to answer.

LAURENT [01/18/07 9:28 PM]

I really want you!!!

But after the billionth message, I thought a reply would be the only way to get him off my back. He hadn't been taking the hint. I really needed a clever plan, but I couldn't contrive one with Pussycat or Special Kay because of the delicate situation. I hadn't told Pussycat about this at all; it didn't seem like they were in touch, but still. Special Kay would certainly not have condoned it. Therefore, this would have to be a covert operation. It just so happened that good old Naughty was coming over for dinner. She was looking for a new apartment, and was thus subletting a dingy place nearby for the time being. Yet, in her time of flux, she was my official roommate (to be able to renew her residence permit). I thought she would serve as the perfect excuse—a pretend overnight guest just when I needed one. I told him I was busy with a "visitor," hoping that would suffice if even for a little while.

LAURENT [01/24/07 2:14 PM]

Hi my blonde! I want you!
I miss you! Kiss

. . .

LAURENT [01/31/07 12:18 PM]

I miss u!!! Kisses everywhere!

I had gained a week or two at best. I just couldn't believe it though: how could he not see that I was trying to brush him off? I'd once been told some wise advice by Lieutenant Steve, which went something like this: *men are like puppies—you have to tell them exactly what to do, how to do it, and be direct. If they are bad, scold them; if they are good, reward them.* Was it really that simple? Somehow, I couldn't manage to muster up enough courage to just say, *"Je ne t'aime pas!"* His not living in Paris helped my cause a little, but he was bound to come back sooner rather than later . . .

LAURENT [02/04/07 10:18 AM]
What do you desire my chérie?

. . .

LAURENT [02/05/07 7:00 PM]
Are you alone on Friday night? If you are,
we could spend the night together! I have
to go to Brittany Saturday morning so
I'm passing through Paris.

This time I really did have Naughty staying with me, having fled the dive she'd been subletting, so it was rather easy to come up with an excuse for not seeing him tonight, and maybe longer.

"How can I get rid of him for good?" I begged her for help.

"Tell him you're pregnant," was her first suggestion. This excuse was often at the top of her list, one I'd never dared use. It would have definitely worked on Valentino; as it was too close to reality for him, he would have run the other way immediately.

"I can't tell him that! He might get jealous and try to track the guy down and kill him or something like that! Or say he wanted to marry me anyway and adopt the kid."

"Tell him you've contracted some kind of rare skin disease." Another bad excuse.

"He'd probably try to come to my side and nurse me back to good health."

LAURENT [02/06/07 12:46 AM]
So can I come over???
I want you so bad!

"Oh, here we go again! See how persistent he is, Naughty?"

By this time we'd had a few glasses of wine and decided to have a little fun with him. Maybe we weren't thinking clearly in our wine haze, and we certainly didn't foresee the consequences of our actions, but we fabricated a message something along the lines of: "I'm not alone, so you can't come over unless you want to have a *ménage à trois*."

LAURENT [02/06/07 01:04 PM]

I don't understand? ménage à trois? It was the chance to spend the night together! Just the two of us! I understand that your friend's there. We can have a drink another time. . . that is unless?

Oh, brother! First of all, we should never have tried to tease him, and certainly not about this! To make matters worse, the French don't even use the same expression! I'd gotten myself into a really sticky mess! The next day the messages came flooding in along with his passionate curiosity . . .

LAURENT [02/06/07 01:08 PM]

Hi darling, is it ok for Friday night? or no? I miss you and you?

So, I had to explain what a *ménage à trois* was, digging our hole even deeper! Now he was totally excited!

LAURENT [02/06/07 01:23 PM]

Would you like to try it together with someone else one day? Another guy? A couple?

. . .

LAURENT [02/06/07 01:42 PM]

Honestly, is it part of your pleasures,
your fantasmes, to be three or more?

I had opened Pandora's box! And the messages didn't stop there. He was like a sex-craved maniac. What was I going to do now? *Fantasme* is the French word for "fantasy," and Laurent definitely did not appear in any of mine!

LAURENT [02/06/07 2:38]

So, no answer, my blonde?

I tried my "not replying" tactic, but I should have realized by then that it had absolutely no effect on him; it only got him more worked up. The messages worsened throughout the day.

LAURENT [02/06/07 3:44 PM]

It could be really nice with
two women or a couple!
. . .

LAURENT [02/06/07 3:52 PM]

2 men with a woman is really orgasmic
for her! Do you have a fantasme?
Several fantasmes? I will do anything to
make them happen for you! I promise!
. . .

LAURENT [02/06/07 3:56 PM]

Tell me your fantasmes! I will make them
come alive in my Heart! Block the next
weekend for me! Very naughty kisses!
. . .

LAURENT [02/06/07 7:01 PM]
What's your fantasmes?

. . .

LAURENT [02/07/07 11:52 AM]
Tell me what you want!

I want you to leave me alone!

After remaining silent for the whole day, I couldn't bear his messages any longer. I sternly replied that I didn't want to share my *fantasmes* with him and that I was NOT free the next weekend. I did stop at, "and I NEVER want to share them with you or see you EVER again," but that *should* have been my final strike. The war was bound to drag on via text message unless I could mount a final assault. But would I have the courage to truly get rid of him?

I'd finally found a "real" French guy who was *crazy about me*, but who, in turn, only *drove me crazy*. It was *je t'aime* multiplied by 1,000,000! This was definitely NOT what I was looking for! But what was it that I was actually looking for now? It seemed that I only found trouble, no matter where I turned. Was I just supposed to give up?

CHRISTAN [03/17/07 02:20 AM]
I got kicked out of the metro by the same
jerk controller... can I still come over?

MELVIN [04/05/07 9:50 PM]
G.nite my lovely lady so nice 2 work with u,
I will move 2 come 2 france 2 c u
one day in my arms. Xx

LAURENT [04/24/07 11:14 PM]
Hi and so for tomorrow? Kisses

LAURENT [04/25/07 2:47 PM]
HI? WHAT ABOUT TONIGHT?

DAVE [05/16/07 6:21 PM]
You are the person I most want to
see, care to meet at the usual?

"Again, you're breaking the poor guy's heart."

"So, you're taking his side? He's the one who at the beginning wasn't sure and wanted to think things over. Just because he's all into me doesn't mean the feelings are mutual."

"You should have told him straight from the beginning that you weren't interested, instead of leading him on."

"I didn't know what to do! At the beginning I actually thought I *might* be interested. And besides, I wasn't really leading him on . . . on purpose. I tried to tell him back in January that I wasn't interested but he obviously didn't get the hint."

"Often you can't just *hint* with men; you need to spell things out loud and clear."

"He must be pretty thick to not have realized that I wasn't interested. I was never free to see him."

"Maybe he thought you were playing hard to get?"

"Very, very hard to get."

"Being in the military, he probably enjoyed the challenge: to crack your code."

"Well, he certainly didn't succeed at that."

"I'm still trying to figure out how to do that. Can you give me any tips?" he pleaded, refilling my glass with one hand and trying to reach out for mine with the other.

"*Umm, Ahhh*, nothing much to know, really."

"Well, I've been trying for two years and haven't managed to gain much territory. I can't handle this anymore! Come home with me tonight, *please!*" I think I finally had no rebuttal for Dave. No clever banter to get out of this one . . .

FROM: DAVE M.   Thursday, 17 May 2007 12:18 AM

Dear Lily,
As usual, I had a great evening. You are so sweet.
Lily, I adore you. Of course you need to find someone closer to your age (and you will), and I need to find someone closer to my age (and I will), but until that happens there is nothing I want more in the world than to hold you against me.

Sometimes I am so overpowered by a longing for you that I feel as if I could die. I do hope we can spend a moment of closeness together. Dave

Over the course of my search for a summer fling, romance, *amour*, whatever I wanted to call it, I did have an eager, available contender for the position. This 'someone' had many of the characteristics I was looking for: a good sense of humor, intelligence, an interesting personality, an international background . . . nevertheless, this anxious suitor had one major disadvantage that was a deal-breaker for me: his age.

Dave and I had met through a mutual acquaintance a few years before. Initially we only saw each other a couple of times through that common friend. However, at an event in the summer of 2005—just at the beginning of my quest—we discovered that we lived in the same neighborhood, so he suggested getting together for a drink sometime—an invitation that seemed innocent enough . . . at the time.

After our third or fourth *apéro* together, Dave suggested going to a concert at a bar he said was nearby. As most of my friends were away on their summer holidays already, I thought, *pourquoi pas?* After accepting his invitation, I found out that the venue was not actually in our *quartier*, but rather in the unsavory part of the 18th district. Though merely a few streets away, it was a great contrast from picturesque Montmartre, and was even worse than the part of the 19th district where Spanish Bobbie lived. I wasn't really positive I felt safe going into no-man's land alone, so we met up at its border and carefully ventured into this dark, possibly dangerous territory. We managed to get to the concert alive; however, it was still daylight, and so getting out of there might be another story.

Entering the dingy (yet cool) bar, we grabbed some glasses of wine and settled down at a table amongst the hipster locals. I must have downed a few more of those glasses pretty quickly to get over the stress of risking my life to get there, and a few more over the reasonably good concert.

I was pleasantly tipsy, but still aware enough to notice that Dave was getting a little flirtatious. In order to enjoy myself, I filed that fact in the back of my mind, though I remained on guard and ready to block him (which was useful for those moments when he touched my arm as he leaned in to say something over the blaring music). Then, upon leaving the bar, he insisted on walking me, not just through the semi-ghetto out to a safe street, but the whole rest of the way home. My protests were silenced and off we went up the hill towards *chez moi*. Here I'd thought the only danger I would have to overcome was getting out of the sketchy area alive. I dodged no bullets—only a shot at my lips from an attempted kiss by Dave instead of a normal *au revoir* kiss on the cheek! This first pass was one of many to come!

Dave actually apologized the next day for his forwardness, and the following times we met up passed without incident. Yet, a different pattern gradually developed: the evenings would get off to a normal start, and then at a given moment, without fail, he would try something. It started with a caress of the arm, which transitioned into trying to hold my hand, and eventually he started trying to get me to stay over at his place . . . or him at mine. He would take whatever he could get!

Now, I know I'm not the best at dealing with these sorts of situations, but I never let things go too carried away. One night, Dave even suggested we date each other until I met someone else. This time, I had to pull out all the stops, as his persistence was getting out of control. So, I said I was looking for someone around my age to settle down with and have a family! *Ha!* Just a little white lie, which I knew would scare him off. It was true that I'd started looking for something more serious, but a good potential dad was not part of my first line of criteria. This caused him to back off . . . for an itsy-bitsy while. When he did start his tactics again, he would eventually remember that I was supposedly looking for "Mr. Father of my Future Children" and would consequently withdraw his advancing hand (or else I would frantically wave at the waiter to get the bill to escape his attempted advances).

Why didn't I just give Dave a try? Despite all of his great features, and the fact that we did have a good time together— he was over 25 years older than me! He'd already been married and had a daughter a few years younger than me!

Admittedly, there are cases of successful and happy couples with a big age difference, but with all the other choices out there floating on the Parisian sea of love, I didn't think see the point in opting for someone so much older. I guess I also just didn't feel there was a *je t'aime* connection between us either. Deep down inside, I wanted to find *l'homme de vie* one day (maybe soon?) and I knew that this was, plain and simply, not Dave. But would he, or at least an interim candidate, materialize before I succumbed to Dave's propositions . . .?

SUMMER LOVE RESOLUTIONS – JUNE

New and improved list and strategy!

Candidate should:

- be smart

- be considerate and nice

- have an international profile (or at least be well-traveled)

- be relatively good-looking, or at least intriguing in some way or another

- be a little older than me (just a *little* — not a LOT!)

- have a good sense of humor

- preferably have some bohemian/artistic tendencies

- have a job other than in a bar

- know how to use a phone, though not chronically

AND don't forget . . .

HE MUST RESIDE IN PARIS

RUSSIAN *ROULETTE*

Yes, somehow summer had once again crept up on me. However, this summer was going to be different—very different. I was sure of it.

I had just watched the international phenomenon *The Secret,* and was determined to alter my fate. In case you are unfamiliar with *The Secret,* it's a 2006 book and movie by Australian author Rhonda Bryne about the law of attraction which puts forth a basic idea: through our thoughts, we attract everything that comes to us. As a strong believer in fate, this theory made sense to me, and I had thus come to the depressing realization that I had attracted all of these oddball, failed romances into my life. It was 100% my fault. *Yikes!* Was I just a sucker for punishment? Despite all of this, it wasn't too late—I could change! Apparently, according to *The Secret,* the way to correct this pattern was to adjust my line of thinking. *Pas de problème!* I could do that!

No more summer *aventure* for me! It was summer, but I wouldn't be seeking out a *fling*, nor would I even be after a little *romance*. Instead, I planned to attract the perfect summer *love*. Maybe even a longer-lasting one at that! This potential person didn't necessarily have to be the final *l'homme de ma vie* (I knew he would come my way at the right time, which may or may not be at this very moment), but I was really ready for an *homme* who might stick around for a little while.

I'd learned from *The Secret* that, in order to get what you want, you have to "secret" it. In short, think about what you want, believe you have it, and it will come. So I thought really hard about the romantic interest I really wanted (but I didn't want to be too picky either!), and I formulated the previously mentioned new "Summer Love Candidate" list. I didn't think I was asking for too much. Plus, it was a list of *positives*, not negatives. I was changing my way of thinking and I was quite confident that, this time, I would get it right and then be able to put my being dumped and all of these misadventures behind me—once and for all.

It was July 1st, and summer had officially started—and a hot one it would turn out to be . . . in more ways than one! The City of Light was morphing into the City of Sweat; the thermometer and the skirt lengths were inching higher day-by-day.

There were a few must-attend events on my annual Parisian calendar, one of my favorites being the Canada Day party at the embassy. The party itself was not necessarily what made it a *must* event—it was rather how we always managed to weave the rest of the evening into an array of chaotic adventures. By starting off at the embassy's official party (with our subsidized Canadian drinks), we got the evening off on the right foot. But once the official bottles of wine and Canadian beer had been emptied, the real party began. Over the past few years, we had developed an unspoken tradition of keeping the patriotic banner waving at the luxurious apartment of the 'fake' ambassador (a particularly entertaining, high-level diplomat who'd earned himself this honorary title), which inevitably included miscellaneous mischief and odd, but memorable characters (who might appear in other stories one day). However, this year we would not be dealt the same hand.

Having made a pact with Naughty to arrive early in order to make the most of the first part of the evening, I waltzed into the courtyard of the embassy at the perfectly acceptable time of 5:15 pm—15 minutes after the doors had opened— and happily picked up my first glass of complimentary wine. I scanned the crowd: Naughty was nowhere in sight, but to my surprise I spotted Lieutenant Steve. What was this workaholic doing there already? More importantly, who was that cute guy he was talking to?

"Steve darling, how did you manage to escape the office so early?" I coyly enquired as I sauntered over to them.

"Well, if it isn't the most popular girl in Paris," he replied, greeting me with a big smile and the *bise*.

"*Ohhh* Steve, that's not true!" I bantered back; I felt as if my cheeks were flushing as red as my glass of wine.

"Sure it is . . . at least with the boys! Oh, by the way, this is Jacques." Before I could continue to defend myself against his claims, I was introduced to the alluring stranger. Steve was always looking to get me into some kind of trouble, and his wife, who usually kept him in check, wasn't there yet!

I was positive that I'd never met the mysterious Jacques before and, as I discovered, neither had Steve, who'd only just befriended him. Steve was also with a third man, whom I'd barely noticed until he began pestering me with nonsensical chatter while I was trying to talk to handsome Jacques. Just as I was about to sink into despair, Naughty appeared, granting me a much needed escape from the third man's creepy conversational clutches.

As the crowd grew, so did our circle of friends, to which Jacques remained attached. I was rather intrigued by this newcomer. I'd instantly noted from his adorable accent that he was French Canadian. *Ooh la la!* I had to fan myself—was it due to the heat of the sun or my increasing inner temperature? I'd been a supporter of Québec and its fight for identity ever since my childhood French school days. I also got to know a few *Québecois* boys more intimately during my student exchange days in Paris, adding to the *mystique* of these *beaux mecs.*

Jacques seemed to be in his mid-30s, and was quite attractive with short, dark hair, and green eyes (oh yes: dangerously green). He was well dressed in a crisp business suit, giving him accentuated I.M.M. appeal. Just as I was rapidly calculating Jacques' dating potential, I caught a glimpse of a handsome silhouette entering the main door. Curious as to who it was, I quickly darted my eyes in the other direction before he noticed that I'd seen him.

It was no stranger this time. It was another attractive man from Montréal . . . none other than Mario, the girlfriend-toting amnesiac from the first summer of my *aventure* quest—and he was at my side in lightning speed. But, I wasn't keeling over with shock at seeing Mario tonight—I'd actually bumped into him the previous week, and indeed that time nearly gave me a massive heart attack (in addition to a week's worth of anguish).

Mario. Oh, Mario. I hadn't seen him in almost a year and a half—not since he'd left my apartment in disgrace after admitting he had a girlfriend. I thought he was lost somewhere in Africa, and that the Parisian coast would be clear of him forever more, but fate works in mysterious ways.

I'd dragged Special Kay to the Saint Jean Baptiste party, otherwise known as the Québec National Day (which bizarrely was exactly one week before Canada Day). Special Kay hated beer and, since that was all they ever served there, she was itching to leave. Plus, the dark, menacing sky looked like it was about to unleash the wrath of the rain gods (you would think from my previous experiences I would have finally started taking this as a sign, a bad omen that something dangerous was about to happen). Impatiently pushing our way through the crowd in an attempt to escape the street party before the ensuing downpour, I ran straight into the tall, dark Mario, leaving me frozen like a caribou in headlights.

"Hey there," he said with an awkward smile.

"Hi . . . Mario, what a surprise . . . Shouldn't you be in Africa?" I managed to blurt out.

"Well, I had a little trouble with all that . . ."

We did our best to make it through some fake small talk, during which I asked if he was going to the embassy next week for Canada Day. He asked me what was going on and I told him to contact me for the details . . . which he did. Special Kay had never met Mario in person. Plus, she didn't exactly have the greatest memory (and besides, it was kind of hard to remember who was who in my Pantheon of boys) so I didn't go into great detail about whom we'd just chatted with. She wouldn't have been impressed at all and would have certainly have lectured me about consorting with him again. It was about then that the first rumblings of thunder boomed through the air, inciting us to careen towards the closest *métro* station, and leave any possible discussion of Mario in the puddles.

Over the course of the next week, I couldn't stop thinking about *why* we'd had that run-in. I deemed it an awfully fateful encounter, just like our first meeting had been almost two years prior. Had I "secret-ed" him back into my life? Was there something in the cards for us after all? Why would anyone sensible have anything to do with this character again? But I wasn't always very sensible . . .

FROM: MARIO W.　　　　Tuesday, 25 June 2007 11:32 AM

Hi Lily, nice bumping into you yesterday. Below are my contact details, drop me a note if you have info on the Canada Day festivities. You mentioned something about the embassy, as well as a party on Saturday?

This year Canada Day fell on a Sunday, a difficult day of the week for celebrations. On the positive side, it allowed us to spread out the various celebratory events: a party at my place on the Saturday night to get a head start; a party on the actual day at our beloved Canadian Bookshop; and an official party held at the embassy on the Monday (the civil servant embassy staff wouldn't work on the weekend).

Mario already had other plans on Saturday and thus couldn't come to the party I was hosting (should I have even invited him in the first place?). However, he was very keen on knowing about the other activities. I gave him the details for the two other parties, and left it at "maybe see you there." I was definitely going to be at both of the other events. I wouldn't want to miss out on a good party; plus, with my new approach to attracting the right summer love, I needed to be in appropriate places for the romance to happen.

The Canadian Bookshop party was also going to feature readings by several authors and one of them just so happened to be runaway train Jake, giving me a double reason to go—and to look as cute as possible. A little red and white top would be perfect—at once patriotic and seductive.

Sunday was a bright and sunny day, allowing the festivities to spill out into the street in front of the bookshop. I arrived on time, accompanied by a French friend: Clém. Jake's reading was well under way when someone came zooming up on a bike: the tall, sporty Mario. My heart skipped a few beats. He came directly over to us, said a cheery hello and didn't budge from my side for the rest of the reading. As Jake described the lively antics of his latest book, Mario gradually edged a little closer to me. When the reading was finished, Mario hung around for a little while, talking only to us, and then biked off as quickly as he'd shown up, allowing my heart to regain its regular pace.

"Who was that?" asked Clém with a smile.

"Oh, he's nothing but trouble," I replied with a sigh, knowing that I would surely see him again.

"He seemed pretty happy to see you," she'd keenly observed. That was just it. It was quite obvious that he'd popped by specifically to see me. He hadn't made an effort to interact with anyone else there, or really check out what was going on. It was all very curious. Would he try his luck again the next day at the embassy?

"Hi there, Lily! You're looking nice," he said, giving me a kiss on the cheek.

"Oh hi, Mario . . . you decided to come!" I exclaimed, with as much surprise as I was able to muster up.

I whipped around to see the astonished, wide-eyed Naughty.

"What is *he* doing here?" she venomously hissed. In fact, that was a very good question: what was he *really* doing there?

He'd arrived a little on the late side, not realizing the embassy party closed up early, so before we knew it, we were all thinking of where to go afterwards. We'd learnt from another staffer that the fake ambassador had been reposted to the Middle East (much harder to throw wild parties there), so tonight there would be no outrageous *soirée* at his place. I had two friends visiting who were on a stopover on their way to Africa (of all places! Maybe they could pack Mario in their suitcase to stop him from complicating my life). So, I thought it might be nice for everyone to go to our new favorite bistro since my booklet launch: *Chez Nicolas*. It was centrally located, so it would be perfect for our next stop . . . and then we could see where the night took us afterwards.

"Do you want to join us, Mario?" I graciously asked.

"Well, I've got my cousin in town, but I'll probably join you guys a little later on; but be sure to keep your phone on so I can find you." And with that he took off.

I turned back to the group and coordinated getting us all to the restaurant. Some wanted to go by *métro*, but in my slight wine haze I thought it would be nice to walk so that my visitors could see more of Paris on their quick stopover. Was anyone else up for a walk? Jacques was still lingering about and expressed an avid interest in continuing the evening with us. He was turning into the wild card of the night, and volunteered to be my walking partner.

We started our route heading south down the luxurious Avenue Montaigne; lined with its designer boutiques, it was the epitome of Parisian chic. This brought us to the Seine, shimmering with the descending sun. Walking east along the river, we came to the most romantic bridge in Paris, Le Pont Alexandre III, ornately decorated with playful river nymphs and guarded on each end by four majestic gilt-bronze Pegasus statues. As we crossed the whimsical bridge, my visitors could also admire the golden dome of Les Invalides on the other side of the river. My friends mostly remained a good 20 paces ahead of us while I gave Jacques a very rough tour of what we were passing, making up any details that I didn't know. He soon caught on and started calling me on the facts.

"How many columns are on that building?" he quizzed, as we approached Assemblée Nationale, the French Parliament with its Greek temple-like façade.

"Eleven," I confidently guessed.

"Why would there be eleven? Looks more like twelve."

"No, no, there are eleven." Wine tends to obscure one's vision.

"Are we almost there?" He pestered.

"Oh, pretty much," I declared, as I steered us down another seemingly endless boulevard (this time it was the Boulevard Saint Germain, known for its historic cafés). Jacques was really funny and kept our stroll peppered with witty jokes. He told me a little more about himself; as it turned out, he was quite an intelligent guy, with a Ph.D. in engineering *and* an MBA. He kept hitting more and more of my summer-love-candidate criteria.

"Are we almost there?" Jacques jokingly repeated, waking me from my dreamy assessment of his potential. He grinned and went on 'complaining' about my supposed short walk, which was turning into a real hiking expedition. We were passing in front of the Eglise de Saint Germain des Près, the oldest church in Paris, its solid main tower still standing after 1,000 years.

"Fret no longer; it's right up this street." Our hike across Paris was actually reaching its end. My guests looked tired, but at least our extended walk had provided them with a perfect crash-course tour of the city. I was almost sad to end our fun stroll, and the lively conversation with Jacques.

Lieutenant Steve, Naughty and Pussycat had already arrived and were seated at a table on the second-floor mezzanine overlooking the bustling main dining room below. We ordered more wine (not like we really needed it), and soon delicious dishes were in front of us, satisfying our hungry bellies after our trek across town. Launching into our dinner, someone suddenly appeared at our table.

"I tried calling, but you didn't answer. I told you to keep your phone on," scolded Mario. I'd honestly totally forgotten that he might be coming; I was having so much fun with Jacques.

"Oops! Sorry about that. Why don't you grab a seat?" I said, completely unapologetically.

He borrowed a seat from a nearby table and stuck it at the end—right between Jacques and me. Mario had ditched his cousin to hang out with us; wasn't that a bit peculiar? I didn't think Mario had noticed Jacques at the embassy, but he was starting to sense he might have a bit of competition. The rest of the evening was rather entertaining, as the two of them vied for my attention like chivalrous knights.

"We can't end the night here," Mario announced as we were finishing up our meals. "It's still early, and it's Canada Day after all! Why don't we go to *The Reindeer*?"

Jeez—I wasn't sure if I was up for seeing Julio, even though after all this time we'd returned to semi-normal friendliness (though I still would have gone out with him in a heartbeat). With these other boys around, I didn't think I could handle a third candidate to flirt with. So, I suggested the other Canadian pub instead. I didn't realize that this might have been an even worse option . . . that's where Mario and I'd made his Oktoberfest bet, which had led to all of our previous trouble. Would there be any new troublesome bets?

So off we went, dragging my poor visitors—who were finally showing their fatigue—to yet another place. At least it really was just a short walk this time.

"You're torturing me with another hike across Paris!" teased Jacques.

"You poor thing, maybe you need a lift?" I sniggered.

Crouching, I offered to give him a piggyback ride, which he accepted, though we didn't make it more than a few steps before tumbling down in fits of giggles. Our physical contact and jovial spirits must have rustled Mario's feathers. Not to be outdone by the competition, he butted in to give *me* a piggyback.

Hold on there! Jacques wasn't about to fold that easily; he fought for shared carrying rights. Soon, I was being jointly carried down the street by two of the cutest Canadian boys in Paris. Both men were very confident with their hands—but who was actually holding the Queen of Hearts?

Arriving at the bar, my candidates continued fighting for my attention, even up until my poor friends began dozing into their beers. So we packed up our decks and headed out to the taxi stand. Parting became a bit awkward, as both knights were trying to play their aces. I definitely wanted to see Jacques again, but I was trying to remember if I'd given him my card earlier at the embassy and, with Mario lingering around, it was virtually impossible to ask. In the end it was Mario who proved himself the best stacked, claiming that as Jacques lived the furthest away in the fancy suburb of Neuilly, he should therefore take the first cab, and with that he almost pushed dear Jacques into the open taxi door. As the cab was driving away, I sighed to myself. *Would I ever see Jacques again?* In my slightly saddened state, I barely said goodbye to Mario when he slid into a second taxi, nor heard his vows to be in touch soon.

After only a few hours of shut-eye, I had to get up to bid my friends a farewell and wish them safe travels to Africa. Luckily, I was just doing some work from home that day; I doubted I would be too intelligent or personable after all the celebratory beverages I'd consumed the previous night. Slugging away at translating an article on the negative effects of drinking on the liver, I instantly perked up at the chime of an incoming text message.

JACQUES [07/03/07 2:55 PM]
Twelve columns . . .

It was Jacques! So I *had* given him my card after all . . . and he wasn't wasting any time in contacting me. Admittedly, my guiding skills hadn't been the best last night under the influence of all that free wine, so I replied with a promise of a better-quality "forced" walk the next time around.

JACQUES [07/03/07 3:13 PM]
But I really like your torture.
More please . . .

Hmmmm, what kind of torture was he seeking? Walking . . . or some other sort of physical task? He definitely seemed eager to see me again, and after a few more text messages, I had confirmed a date with him for the following evening.

That was easy! I was actually a little excited. Jacques increasingly seemed to be the perfect fit for my summer *amour*. However, as the much-needed coffee was finally starting to kick in, my brain was waking up to some details from our previous night's conversation. From what I could recall, Jacques had said something about how he worked in Moscow, but came to Paris fairly frequently. That wasn't ideal—it actually contravened one of my repeating resolutions about only accepting someone residing in Paris. However, he appeared to have a full house of the other qualities I was looking for and, after two years of being less than ideal in the romance department, I was now prepared to take my best offer, which in this case might just be a travelling *amoureux*. Besides, after my last few escapades, I definitely didn't want anyone too clingy anyway (Laurent had *finally* realized I wasn't going to respond to his text messages and had abandoned the battlefield), and dating a North American, long-term European resident might just be the best match. Indeed, he seemed the best of both worlds. *Hmmm*, I'd never been to Moscow before . . . getaway weekends to Russia were a rather appealing possibility for a summer romance!

At first, I didn't think it was too strange that Jacques wanted to meet up at 9:30 pm, which was certainly later than the normal time for a first date. I figured he probably had a late work meeting and was squeezing me into his busy schedule. We met facing l'Arc de Triomphe at the center of l'Etoile, the large star-shaped roundabout at the far end of the Champs-Elysées, which was metaphorically (and geographically) a very romantic place to start our evening. I was under the impression that we would be going for a drink (as people do on first dates), so I'd chosen to wear appropriate attire and sexy heels to fit in at one of the area's posh cocktail lounges. But Jacques hadn't been joking about going for a forced walk across Paris; he was dressed a bit casually, with jeans and running shoes, apparently ready for a new hike (at 9:30 pm?)! I would have to see how long my feet would hold up in the heels . . .

We started strolling down the world famous Avenue des Champs-Elysées, emblazoned with a lovely golden glow from the setting sun. As we walked, Jacques told me a little bit more about what he did, which I didn't fully grasp . . . something like investment banking or real estate development. I gathered that it involved helping rich Russians invest their money—in any case, I deemed it exciting and probably a little dangerous!

Our conversation and laughter seemed to echo off of the ornate buildings. He was full of the same quirky humor from the other night and I added to the fun atmosphere by mixing up the facts and figures of some sites we passed. With all the merriment, I'd hardly noticed that we'd made it all the way down the long street and were at the beginning of the Tuileries Garden (previously visited with another traveling love interest—Dean, the pilot). Normally closed in the evening, part of the garden was open that night, hosting a sort of mini fun fair. This would not usually be my cup of tea, yet both Jacques and I were mesmerized by its largest attraction: a colossal, illuminated Ferris wheel.

"Want to give it a try?" he asked, pointing to the huge, dangerous-looking structure.

"The view must be great. We'll be able to see all of Paris and continue our tour from up there," I joked. But before I could even finish my sentence, Jacques was at the ticket counter.

I am a *tad* afraid of heights, and the old rickety wheel didn't make me feel very reassured; however, once we got to the top, the view made any fear vanish. We really could see all of Paris, and what a magical vista it was! I was in awe at the twinkling lights of the city, dancing along the rooftops; and, as if on cue, the Eiffel Tower burst out into its spectacular hourly sparkling show. What a romantic setting; it would have been the perfect moment for a kiss . . .

Back on solid ground, we continued our evening hike in the direction of Île de la Cité, the tall towers of Notre Dame Cathedral guiding our way. Crossing over one of the ancient Pont Neuf, we stopped to admire the shimmering river. Of course, this was another very picturesque place in Paris— especially designed for embracing lovers. This time, Jacques took action and fulfilled the bridge's *raison d'être* with an intense kiss.

At last! I had a summer romance getting off to a solid good start! I was in amorous seventh heaven! Strolling along the mysterious streets of Old Paris, on the arm of an attractive, intelligent guy . . . perhaps this was all too good to be true? The whole situation *did* seem perfect . . . that was until Jacques started making odd comments.

"That looks like a nice hotel, maybe we should go check it out?" he suggested with a coy smile. *Had I hear him correctly?* No, I couldn't have. However, his sly suggestion came up again when we passed the next hotel . . . and the one after that, bringing back unpleasant memories of having to dodge indecent innuendoes on that little Normandy jaunt with my student Jean-Claude.

We soon found ourselves walking alongside Notre Dame, at which point he made a subtle suggestion to sneak into the garden, followed by a kiss on the cheek. I wanted to just brush this off as his being silly; he really *had* to be joking, but this time his jokes weren't making me laugh. Receiving no sign of agreement on my part, he suggested stopping at a café for a drink, and his peculiar comments thankfully faded. Finally, it was about time! I'd been swept away in the lofty ambience; I hadn't really noticed how much my feet were killing me, what with them being confined in my inappropriate foot-wear. We grabbed a table facing the peace cathedral; the graceful panorama and much-needed break from all the walking helped push his peculiar remarks to the back of my mind—for a short while. After finishing our drinks, Jacques started making little hints about coming home with me. There was *nooo* way I was going to give in to that— I was playing this one by the books.

He accompanied me in a taxi up to my neighborhood, as it was "on his way home," probably in the hopes of changing my mind. However, I stuck to my guns. When we reached my street, I gave him a last kiss goodnight before exiting the vehicle and entered my building resolutely alone. I knew that I'd made the right move; nevertheless, I tossed and turned in bed, thinking long into the night. He'd be going off to Spain in a few days, and then where would he be headed? When would he be coming back to Paris? The big question I began asking myself was: *did* I even want to see him again? I'd been left with such uncertainty. Even though he had gotten a little weird towards the evening's close, after all of this mental debate, the romantic sucker in me won out, trying to keep positive about this *possible* summer love. I was still in a confused state when I received a surprising phone call the following week.

"Hey there Lily, it's Mario." *Oh God*, what did he want? I'd practically forgotten about him.

He proposed having lunch, but I was more than a little suspicious about the real motives behind his invitation. He even offered to come up to my neck of the woods, making me all the more wary. Perhaps sensing my reticence, he added that he was curious to see how I'd done up my place. Ah yes, that was right. He was the first person who'd

seen it, empty with growing piles of boxes as I was moving in
. . . just before he'd told me he had a girlfriend! Those
particular bad memories were from the days of my old place,
so it probably wouldn't cause me any harm to have him stop
by. So, I amicably agreed to a lunch date for the next Friday.

After a quick tour of my place (staying clear of the mirrors
so he wouldn't be possessed to do the same eye-color stunt
that he had the first time he tried to seduce me), we went
down to the bustling rue des Abbesses for lunch. We settled
in at my local café and perused the menu. Awaiting our
déjeuners, the conversation wasn't too awkward, despite our
unfortunate history. In all honesty, he'd occupied a painful
place in my heart this whole time. I had been so disappointed
by fate the last time around and still completely bewildered
that nothing was meant to be between us that I'd lost any and
all reasonable judgment or skepticism in his regard.

I listened as he told me how his plans to work in Africa
had been foiled by local officials, though he was still hoping
to make it back there in the near future. To succeed at this,
he'd quit his job and was looking for a new one—this being
the reason he could take time during the day to have lunch up
in Montmartre. *Sigh!* Even if he did show real interest in me
this time, was there any point in wishing for anything to
happen between us if he was just going to disappear off
to Africa?

By the end of the meal, he'd ventured into some different
conversational territory.

"So, are you seeing anyone?" he hesitantly asked.

Even if I didn't have an "official" boyfriend, I wasn't
going to tell *him* that. Then again, why was he asking? Was he
interested? I needed to respond proudly, while also leaving

the door potentially open . . . for him.

"Well, I'm kind of seeing this French guy, but I don't really know if it's going to work." This was open-ended enough and actually wasn't a complete lie—and this French guy wasn't Jacques. I didn't want him to know that something might be brewing with Jacques; it was too soon to tell where that particular relationship was going, and it was none of Mario's business anyway. But I had a different "pretend" boyfriend in my back pocket. The "French guy" I was referring to was a guy I'd met at a party the previous month (before meeting Jacques and running into Mario) who was so horribly pathetic he barely deserves to be mentioned and can be summed up in the following equation: offered ride home - towed car + Lily paying for taxi = I.O.U. dinner x loser calling frequently but never leaving voicemail to book date ÷ the fact that he brought all his friends to dinner = Lily paying for her own dinner and never calling him back ever again.

"And what about you?" I felt forced to reciprocate the question, even though I sort of didn't want to know the answer.

"Well, I'm actually still with the same girl."

What? I almost spit out the mouthful of wine I'd just taken to ease my nerves. He was still with the same girl—a year and a half after cheating on her with me (and possibly other girls?). Either he was a total coward or she was an evil dominatrix. I was betting on option A (but hey, she was French, so it could have been a combination of both!).

What could I say to that? Of course, I was too shocked to come up with any brilliant lines such as: *Wow, I can see why you stayed with her! She must be fabulously understanding or completely blind to put up with your cheating!* Or maybe: *So, how many other girls have you made "bets" with?* Or better yet: *You're a really lame piece of crap.* I was just too nice (and stunned) to say any of the nasty things he deserved to hear. I might have managed a slight, "that's pathetic" look, or an "oh really" raised-eye brow, but not much else.

He went on a little rant about the challenges of dating someone of another nationality: you're not always on the same wave-length, you have different ways of thinking, etc. I was totally baffled. If he was unhappy 18 months ago, what was he still doing with her? Nevertheless, as I mentioned above, my common sense had disappeared and through all the *blah, blah, blah,* the one thing that my mind retained was that he seemed to finally be on the verge of ending things with the other girl. Perhaps Mario was hanging out with me in order to escape his girlfriend . . .? Since he wasn't going off to Africa just yet, could he be looking for a different getaway excuse? Wasn't it strange how we kept bumping into each other? Was fate trying to bring us together again? I wanted so desperately to believe that this could happen, though our first chance-encounter years ago had left some dark clouds hanging over my opinion of Mario (as it should have!).

He suspiciously paid for lunch as well. Was this merely due to left-over guilt, or was it a seductive first attempt to re-conquer me? In return, I took him on a bit of a casual tour of the area, full of witty (and factually-correct) commentary. He seemed happy to be spending time with me. Our time together was going so well, but true to our nebulous history, our potential horizons were darkening by actual encroaching clouds, cutting short our tour. He dashed off as the first raindrops fell, skimming my cheek with a kiss and vaguely suggesting that we get together sometime soon.

Even though my heart might have quivered a bit over our lunch, for the time being, Mario would have to cohabitate it with my adorably-accented banker to the Russian mafia (alright, maybe a slight exaggeration of his job, but why not heighten the excitement?). Jacques was still in first place in this romantic race. Well, technically girlfriend-laden Mario wasn't even an official contender and, as the joyful sun of the beginning of July was slowly being washed away by weeks of wind and rain, so were thoughts of Mario . . . until I received a surprise call from him at the end of the month.

"Are you going on the hike next Sunday?" he inquired, a handy excuse for calling.

Ha! Was I going on the hike? My days of contemplating attending Canadian Club hikes in the mere hope of seeing him were long past.

I stammered out my various excuses for not going, bidding him a happy meander in the wet woods, and we signed off. We were actually having a little party on the eve of the hike, so there was no chance in Parisian *enfer* that I was going to get my butt out of bed at the crack of dawn to go traipsing through the forest.

Hmmm, you might not be going on the hike, but maybe Mario would like to come to the party instead? said the little devil who'd materialized on my shoulder. *What? Why would you want to do that?* piped up the little angel rationally on the other shoulder. The angel was right: I shouldn't be inviting him to social events. However, the little devil's voice stuck around in my head, and pestered me for a day or two until I finally gave in. I picked up my cell, scrolled through my call log for his unsaved number (in a venomous rage, I'd deleted him from my phone contacts right after the first girlfriend-admitting episode), and invited him to join us. By then, he'd already made plans to go on the hike with some other friends. I wished them luck—they would need it, as the dismal weather forecast was calling for rain . . . yet again. And so I re-shelved any and all ideas of Mario, and turned my mind to the fact that sexy Jacques was coming to town.

Hurrah! My summer love plans were back on the right track! My wistful mind had started dreaming of several days of romantic bliss . . . that is, until I found out that he'd only be in Paris for one night. While way too short a time, at least he was saving that one night for me. Maybe I could suggest a little visit to Moscow to see him while he was here?

JACQUES [08/08/2007 7:31 PM]

Salut ma Tigresse. Just taking off from Moscow, should be on time. Will call when I arrive.

As promised, he called upon arriving at Charles de Gaulle airport. Since he would have to go home to drop off his bag, we set our meeting point for 9:30 pm outside of the *métro* station near his place in Neuilly. I cheerfully got ready, put on an attractive evening ensemble, one classy enough for his uppity neighborhood, yet smartly layered to withstand the unpredictable sky. What would the night have in store for us? I gave myself a final check-over in the mirror and scooped up an umbrella on the way out the door.

Exiting the *métro*, I instantly found handsome Jacques awaiting me. He greeted me with a big smile and a kiss on the cheek.

"Are you hungry?" he asked.

"Not really," I answered. As it was fairly late, I'd already eaten, thinking we were just going for a drink.

"I haven't eaten, so do you mind if I grab something?" he pursued.

"Of course not," I responded sweetly. A girl should never utter this sort of reply before asking: *"Where did you have in mind?"* I'd just assumed we were going to one of the many chic cafés lining the streets of Neuilly, where I could get a glass of wine and he could have a *steak-frites* or something like that. But instead, I was being ushered into a certain appalling fast food chain. Was this another Jacques joke?

No, he wasn't kidding around this time; I was soon the best-dressed person inside this particular branch of the *McDo* golden arches. Maybe he literally wanted to "grab" something and gobble it down quickly before going elsewhere for a proper drink date?

Once he had finished his fat-saturated burger and fries— and I, a few sips of a watery soda—Jacques suggested going for a walk. He was turning out to be a more active hiker than Mario! I wasn't sure if that was such a great idea, not only due to my inappropriate attire, but also due to the fact that it was also now 10:30 pm, hardly the time for a huge hike around the city. And besides, where was there to walk to in Neuilly . . . in the dark? As much as I didn't like his proposition, I wasn't going to be a wimpy complainer; I'd play along and go on his stroll. I didn't know Neuilly very well; I supposed this would give me the chance to see the city a little. However, as we ventured down a few blocks lined with elegant centuries-old mansions, the beauty was overshadowed by some startling conversation from Jacques.

"Don't you have a few husbands somewhere? Haven't you ever been married?" he casually joked. *What were these odd questions all about?*

"Ha, ha, I'm too young!" I nervously laughed. *Married?* I looked over at him, trying to gauge his level of seriousness.

"What about you?" I felt I had to reciprocate his awkward male question, harking back to the maladroit moment over lunch with Mario. Did I even want to know the answer to my forced question? There was a thick layer of dread hanging in the normally peaceful Neuilly evening air.

"Actually, I'm also Spanish." That wasn't exactly a direct answer to my question, but it served as a way of learning some things about his past and *how* he'd come to be Spanish. It turned out that Mr. Quebec-meets-Russia-via-France had a bit of a secret background, which I would discover slowly over the next few months, like piecing together a complex puzzle. After a bit of verbal digging around, I got to the roots of his dual nationality—he'd been married to a Spanish woman . . . for ten years!

"Are you *still* married?" I couldn't help blurting out.

"No, not to her, but we have a daughter together."

Well, well, well, now *that* explained why he went to Spain on occasion . . . and here I thought it was for business! I supposed it could have been worse. Better a divorced wife and family in Spain than a current one here. I wasn't sure if I wanted to be a step-mother-like figure any time in the long-foreseeable future. However, being tucked away in Spain, his daughter didn't really pose a problem to Jacques and I seeing each other.

With all this confusing marriage/family/kid talk, I hadn't realized that our stroll was leading us into the beginnings of the Bois de Boulogne, the large woods to the west of Paris, famous for great jogging paths by day . . . and transvestites by night. Before coming out there, I hadn't thought I'd be running into prostitutes in drag, but my day was turning out to be full of surprises!

It might have been because of the fresh scent of the forest, or perhaps it was the sexual vibes emanating from the *Bois*, but whatever the cause, Jacques started putting on some very serious moves.

"Maybe we should head back to civilization?" I timidly suggested, trying to stave off his ravenous advances. Maybe it was common practice to make out in the bushes in Québec (at night!), but it was far from my idea of romantic.

Luckily, he didn't insist too much. However, heading back into the center was also an excuse for Jacques to invite me over to his place, which was conveniently only a few blocks away—in a safer direction than the one we'd been taking towards the woods.

Frankly, I was very confused. I had no idea what I was supposed to think about Jacques and things were about to get ever foggier. *A Spanish wife and kid? Should I even be going over to his place?* A looming dread had settled over our evening, but by then we were approaching a nice, modern building on a quiet, tree-lined street, and Jacques was acting more normal. I felt like I had things under control.

We entered the building and approached one of the ground floor apartments. He pulled out his keys, unlocked the door, and I followed him inside. From the entrance I immediately couldn't help but notice a clutter of colorful objects. Was that a little tricycle? A mini-chair? *A giant teddy bear?*

Bewildered, I found more of the same upon entering the living room. I thought he had a *tween* who lived in Spain. Had he just not gotten rid of her old belongings? In a quick scan around the room, I spotted all sorts of Japanese things: books, decorations, Hello Kitty merchandise. My gaze halted on a pile of documents on the counter. Was that a Japanese passport and ID card ... *of a woman?* I didn't think I'd heard wrong earlier on . . . he had indeed said *Spanish* wife. And the words Spanish and Japanese do NOT sound remotely similar in English OR in French. What was going on? Was Jacques really a transvestite Russian/Japanese spy? As I was about to ask for some clarification, Jacques attempted to distract me.

"Can I get you something to drink?" he offered, discretely sliding the passport under an envelope. "*Hmmm* . . . it seems there's only pineapple juice. I'm not here very much. Look, even the plants are dying!"

So was he saying that *nobody* was ever here, or just not *him?* The former could be possible, in the same vein as the barman François, who'd kept his ex-girlfriend's things around for over a year after their break-up.

But what was all this Japanese stuff about? Sneaking a better look at the photos on the walls, it seemed like there was a cute little JAPANESE girl in many of them—possibly the owner of the *tricycle?*

"Life is complicated," he joked. "Isn't yours?"

"Certainly not as complicated as YOURS!" I had to say.

That was all the commentary I was granted at that time. Jacques slyly changed the subject and continued his charming act between sips of pineapple juice, leaving me no chance to ask about the Japanese connection.

I do have to say there was fairly strong attraction between

us. I let my now extreme desire to succeed at my summer love mission take control. Why would Jacques be pursuing me if he still lived with this Japanese companion . . . and child? Maybe, whoever they were, they'd left ages ago and, since he was never there, he just hadn't gotten around to getting rid of their things? Obviously, he was free to see me . . . *right?*

But before I could rehash my doubts, I was being kissed by Jacques and carried off to a full-sized grown-up bed. Wasn't I supposed to be living in the moment? I truly wanted to embrace this attempt at a summer romance, and so I did. Night quickly turned into morning and someone had to head off to the airport.

Where was he going this time? I'd previously assumed he was off on another business trip, but now I wasn't sure because he was going to . . . Japan. Why was he going there? Was he visiting his FAMILY? A repeated "Life is complicated" was his only consolation, accompanied by another promise that he might be going to Canada on holiday approximately when I would also be there in a few weeks' time, and he'd do his best to see me there.

I walked down the street, heartbroken. If he was going to Japan, it most certainly meant that he was still "with" the Japanese woman in some form or another. Maybe he'd bought the ticket ages ago and then their relationship deteriorated after that? *Nah,* that was unlikely. Maybe he was also doing some business there? That option was potentially credible, but still a little far-fetched. The facts and theories were getting all muddled up in my mind. The only thing I was certain about was that I felt terribly *sad.* How could I have just trusted him, without asking more questions?

This wasn't at all what I'd been hoping for or what I had "secret-ed." This wasn't a summer *amour* at all—it was a summer *mess*.

"What ever happened to Jacques?" questioned Naughty. "Where's he this time?"

It was now the end of August and the girls and I were catching up after our respective holidays. I was trying to keep the bizarre situation with Jacques under wraps. If they knew the real story, I would surely get a downright (and well-deserved) scolding.

"*Wellll*, I'm not really sure. He said something about going to Japan . . . *umm*, for work . . . then to Canada," I fudged. He'd probably already come and gone from both destinations. He'd barely been in touch this last month, only just recently to say that he was going to Canada later than expected and our dates wouldn't overlap after all. I forced myself to believe him, despite that sneaky little devil who was hanging about, taunting me about the situation. He'd invented all kinds of stories featuring Jacques at some relaxing lakeside cottage, holidaying with both his Japanese and Spanish families. I had to push those thoughts out of my mind. Another glass of *Saint Amour* would help me forget my woes.

"Jeez, is he *ever* in Paris?" grilled Special Kay.

"Maybe I should move on . . . forget about Jacques entirely," I sighed, on the verge of conceding romantic defeat yet again.

As the girls started nodding their heads in unison agreement, my phone rang. I looked down at the screen, hoping to see Jacques' name light up the screen so I could prove them all wrong. Instead it was someone even worse in their books . . . the wishy-washy, tied-down Mario (I'd re-saved his number in my phone, but truly only so I could be prepared when he called). *Yikes!* What did he want? The phone went on ringing while I contemplated answering or not.

"Hello?" I gave in on the fourth ring.

"Hey there, Lily. How are things?" Did I mention that Mario had this incredibly sexy hint of a Dutch accent? Maybe even more melt-worthy than Jacques'? It was very easy to fall under his verbal spell. We chatted rather cheerily about the holidays, and this and that, until he finally got around to his point.

"So, I've got some good friends coming to town this weekend. What are you guys up to?"

"Actually, we're going to an international party on a boat. It should be fun. You're welcome to join us with your friends," my sentence immediately sparking wide eyes and waving hands from the girls. I would get a scolding tonight after all.

"Did you really just invite him out with us?" exclaimed Special Kay as soon as my finger had pressed the "end" button on my phone.

"You know, Lily, that might not have been such a good idea," chimed in the normally neutral Pussycat.

"Can that cheating liar ever be trusted again?" Naughty interrogated.

"Can't we just put the past behind us? So far he's been

good this time around," I said weakly, in an attempt to defend both Mario and my good judgment. Yet, I was defeated by the rightful skepticism of the girls.

Was Mario hedging some new bets? It wasn't fair to assume he had any ulterior motives, other than simply looking for a fun night out with his visitors. Even though he'd taken the initiative to contact me this time, I'd given him the go-ahead for social interaction when I'd invited him out with us back at the end of July. Here we were, a month later, and now the little fluttering hearts for Jacques were tempted to fly away with the warm summer days. Mario's increasing interest in "hanging out" together made me seriously wonder if he had finally ditched his ball-and-chain of a girlfriend and was thus free to pursue me; but, fearing retribution from *les filles*, I thought it best to keep these theories to myself.

Wearing a sequined royal blue top, a wavy black skirt and a huge smile, off I went to the boat party. All the girls were there, plus our personal bodyguard, Lieutenant Steve. We got there on the early side to make the most of the two-for-one drink special and free buffet. The temperature was still quite mild, so we found some seats next to some Italians on the upper deck. Mario and his friends eventually showed up and he seemed more than eager to distract me from the friendly Italians. Another round of two-for-one drinks? Don't mind if I do!

And around and around came those rounds of drinks, with Steve and Mario taking turns keeping our table well-stocked with cocktail glasses. The atmosphere was picking up, and being sufficiently warmed up by our bottomless drinks, we made our way to the dance floor. Burning off some of that alcohol was probably a good idea. So far, the night was going brilliantly and we were all having a great deal of fun. Naughty had found her own target (a cool gent sporting a hat); Special Kay kept scanning the crowd for a prince in shining armor (to no avail); and Pussycat friendlily boogied with Steve. Who did that leave me with?

There comes a point of no return in most evenings, usually late into the *soirée*, when built-up sexual tension can no longer be contained. Mario had gradually been moving towards me, closer and closer, until we were once again eye-to-green-eye. The girls seemed too busy (or tipsy) to spot this at first, but it was hard not to notice when he started kissing me. Mario had descended for his kill and I was willing prey. It almost seemed like time was standing still. Had we turned back the clocks two years, or were we picking up from where we had left off? Mario was quite content with his prize—as I was with mine—and didn't leave my side (or my lips) . . . until he realized that his friends were falling asleep at our table. Their jet lag was setting in and it was time for them to leave. I was asked if I'd be going with them. Maybe I wasn't even asked, but since I was clutching Mario's arm, it was assumed that I would be leaving at the same time. However, *where* were we going?

Leaving the boat, we helplessly wandered around in pursuit of a taxi (a doomed quest on a Saturday night). Starting to lose hope, we switched gears and went in search of some *Velibs,* the city's shared rental bikes. Yet, when we finally found a station, there weren't enough bikes for all of us (which was probably a good thing—considering the quantity of beverages we'd consumed, biking home might not have been the safest idea). Miraculously, just then, a cab pulled up to save us—just one.

"*Vous allez où?*" asked the cabbie. A quick compromise was worked out; we'd first take the taxi to drop the friends off at Mario's place in the east of Paris, and then we'd go north to my place—the latter "we" being Mario and I.

A wave of trepidation swept over me. *Is this such a good idea?* questioned the angel. *Of course it is!* energetically asserted the wily devil. *With those moves, he's obviously broken up with his girlfriend*, the little troublemaker added. Remembering that Mario had alluded to ending the relationship during our July lunch conversation, I chose to side with the devil. After all, Mario had been after me ever since our run-in last June. In addition to quieting the angel, I blocked out visions of the girls shaking their heads and waving their arms in caution and exasperation, warning me to watch out; instead, I let myself enjoy having won Mario back.

Mario and I barely slept a wink; he was just as sexy as before. Even though the next day was a Sunday, I had to work rather early in the morning, which meant trekking across town to give a private English class. Crawling out of bed with my throbbing head, and leaving the arms of my all-too-recently-reacquired-prize was agony, but the idea of FINALLY hitting the jackpot kept me going. Plus, when I hadn't wanted to get up, Mario had whispered, "Don't worry, there will be other times." That was enough to keep me going for the next few hours, in addition to reassuring me that true romance was really going to spark this time. We parted ways in front of the *métro* with a soft kiss and an "I'll call you soon" promise.

Mario was about to go on a bit of a road trip, so I actually didn't expect to see or hear him in the immediate future. That's why I was totally surprised to see his number flashing on my ringing phone a few days later.

He was driving along the highway and needed someone to talk to about life and his career impasse. Well, wasn't it nice to be considered a good person to turn to in his time of need? The conversation "re-stoked" my hopes for a little longer. He'd be back soon and would call me again, right?

Oddly, the next interesting phone call I got wasn't from Mario . . . it was from Jacques.

It seemed that he hadn't forgotten about me, after all. To tell you the truth, I hadn't really forgotten about him either, although I was still very confused . . . and Mario's brief reappearance in the picture did complicate matters, just a tiny bit. Even though I was very happy that things might be headed along the right track with Mario, he hadn't made me any promises and so I was free to see Jacques . . . and hopefully get to properly assess our situation.

He was only going to be in town for a couple of days (*big surprise!*) but had managed to find some time for me in his busy schedule. However, just like the previous occasions, our time together wasn't a typical date. Jacques told me that he would be going to Africa in December to climb Mount Kilimanjaro; therefore, he needed to train.

Erroneously thinking I was some big hiking fan, he suggested going for a day-long forest promenade. *Uggh!* It wasn't quite my idea of fun, but since it was the only day we could see each other, I wasn't in a position to be picky— or reveal my real lack of interest in sports! So I put on a brave face and cheerfully accepted to go. Regardless of the activity, I was looking forward to spending the whole day together— it would give me a chance to get some answers out of him. He couldn't very well escape from my prying questions if we were deep in the woods!

Maybe it was just because of the excellent company, but the hike wasn't as torturous as I'd thought it would be. We went to the beautiful Fontainebleau forest (yes, the same Fontainebleau where Laurent the *gendarme* often worked. I doubted we'd run into him in the forest, unless his unit was conducting some search and rescue practice). Even though it wasn't that far from Paris, it felt a world away from the hustle and bustle of the city. Over the course of our wet day, I procured more and more pieces of his intricate puzzle.

I found out that he'd married the Spanish woman when he was only 24. She was seven or eight years older than he was, and within a few years of married life along came his *first* child. Without his totally admitting it, I gathered that he'd started a liaison with the Japanese woman while he was still with his Spanish wife. He'd probably thought that he'd met a cute, young, innocent Asian to have his own racy fling with. However, when the Japanese woman got accidentally pregnant, Jacques was forced to leave the marriage that was ending and moved in with the Japanese woman, who turned out to be the exact same age as the Spanish wife and had a husband she'd left behind in Japan! Things with her rapidly began to deteriorate and—according to Jacques—she turned a little psychotic. So, he had run off to work in Moscow early this year, and later fatefully met me at the embassy back in July. *Voilà.* That about summed it up. Jeez, was he trying to line himself up with a U.N. General Assembly of Women?

I was really, and at the moment literally, stuck between a rock and a hard place. I was very fond of Jacques; however, he hadn't been fully honest from the beginning. I wanted to believe that he really wasn't "with" the Japanese woman and was merely supporting her, for the child's sake. While this could very well have been true, I wasn't convinced that it made sense to continue seeing Jacques with his random appearances in Paris; the lack of assurance that he wasn't with the Japanese woman; and the lack of promises about us. It wasn't going to be an easy decision to make, but since he'd be back in Moscow for a while before heading off to Africa, I had plenty of time to make up my mind.

As my mind was debating Jacques, I was conveniently distracted by a certain Dutchman. He suggested getting together for lunch. That was a good start, but a lot was at stake this time: how was I going to make sure I would win him over for real?

"Well, if he's invited you for lunch, then it seems like he's into you," rationalized Cindy, who'd been out with us the night I'd met intensely-romantic Valentino. She was in town on business, so I used the occasion to get a new perspective on my romantic dilemmas. The other girls would be flat out against any plans of me meeting up with Mario. Plus, Cindy was also quite skillful in playing her cards right, case in point being her latest (and last) victory: a hot younger guy who fell head-over-heels for her (and who became her future husband!). If anyone could help me succeed, it was Cindy.

"But you can't let him get the upper hand," she duly advised. "Most importantly, when you are finishing up lunch, you have to try to leave suddenly; this will throw him off his game and make him want you more." *I could do that!*

I began choreographing my moves, and was eventually ready to pull my trump out at just the right moment. On the day of my lunch-date with Mario, I had classes in the morning then another one in the late afternoon, which would serve as my excuse to briskly leave at the right time. I would be coy and smart, though not overly nice, and I couldn't suggest meeting again; he would have to put that forward.

MARIO [10/25/2007 11:45 AM]

Sorry Lily, I'm still helping my friends move. Can we make it a coffee a little later instead of lunch?

Just a coffee? *Hmmpf!* Well, something was better than nothing; I hadn't seen him in ages! I kept my cute composure and headed off to our new designated meeting point for coffee at 3:30 pm. I arrived a reasonable five minutes late, but there was no sign of Mario. Any hopes of carrying out the Cindy's advice were being thwarted from the get-go. Mario showed up about ten minutes later, all grubby from helping his friends . . . grubby—but still completely adorable.

We settled in at the cozy Café Hugo, in the normally tremendously romantic Place des Vosges, the very same place I'd had lunch with Jake last year, when he first confessed to his own recurring girlfriend. I was trying not to think of that dreaded lunch; this was not lunch, after all, this was coffee. Well, the "coffee" ended up turning into a glass of wine . . . but by then it was going on 4:00 pm—a very respectable "*apéro*/quell-one's-nerves" time.

We hadn't seen each other since the time he'd stayed over, nor had we ever talked about what had happened. On this sunny autumn afternoon, we opted for cheery conversation sprinkled with a few compliments from Mr. Gorgeously Grimy about how nice I looked, causing my heart to flutter. He told me about his little road trip and his recent job interviews (one based in Paris, that instantly lifted my spirits!). After about 45 minutes, I attempted to follow Cindy's stern advice: to suddenly dash off.

"Well, nice seeing you, Mario. I really have to go," I exclaimed after he'd paid the bill, grabbing my purse and standing up with quick determination, while trying to remain as calm, cool, collected and seductive as possible.

"Which way are you headed?" he unexpectedly asked.

"Towards the Seine," I replied hesitantly, wishing a hot air balloon could land in the square at that very second and whisk me safely away before I did anything stupid.

"I'll walk with you," he offered, totally foiling my carefully crafted plans. *Uggh,* I was impossible. How could I say no? Where was my teleportation device?

"Okay, I guess that's fine, but I don't have much time." I would try to stick as much to my rapidly unraveling ploy as possible; I could lose him down one of the Marais narrow alleyways.

I tried to further charm him with my knowledge of the area as we walked towards the *métro* line I needed to catch. The further we walked, the weirder Mario started acting; it was almost as if he was anxious about something. Why would he be nervous? I was acting as nonchalant as possible. I blah-blahed away until we were almost at the station, when he finally got up enough courage to speak.

"I have to talk to you about something . . ." *Ughh!* Something to talk about always meant something bad.

"I had a really great time with you after we went out the last time, and I'd really like it to happen again, but . . ."

But *what?* My stomach started churning, and a glance at my watch said I had about two minutes before I needed to be sitting on that *métro* car.

". . . but I'm still with my girlfriend."

Had I heard him correctly? I was dumbstruck. He hadn't ditched the French cast-iron anchor after all. What a pathetic wimp! Either that, or he really did have a serious case of sporadic amnesia as I'd thought the first time around. This twist completely threw off all my plans, disarming Cindy's advice that I'd vowed—and earnestly attempted—to follow. While I was standing there in utter disbelief, Mario embarked on a long rant about how things were complicated with the French girl and weren't going well, and that they might break up, and how he really wanted to sleep with me again . . . *out of lust.*

"So what do you think?" was his selling line.

What do I think? Did he really say just "out of lust"? I had no idea what I was I supposed to say to his proposition. Any clear thinking girl would have probably told him to go to hell, but I was so confused and running out of time that all I managed to spit out was: "I'll think about it," an answer that I should have known to be dangerous from the mistress-hunting episode with Jean-Claude, though today it earned me a quick kiss on the lips and a promise to be called soon.

Out of lust? Did that mean he couldn't care less about me? Did my charm and wit have no effect on him? On the *métro* I attempted to understand our conversation. Somewhere near the beginning of it, I recalled an, "I don't know where things are going with my girlfriend . . . she probably won't be my girlfriend for long."

This was something for my hope to cling to. My optimism convinced my good-judgment that I could still win him over. How could he not want to end that obviously dead-end relationship? Why not jump ship if it was sinking? I'd soon managed to refashion his proposition into something almost acceptable. I gave the girls a slightly edited version of the story, leaving out the end (for fear of being completely disowned and banned from dating for even considering such a proposal). I pondered the situation deeply. I couldn't get it out of my mind that fate had thrown us together. And if I needed any more convincing, I had the old, "well, this is better than nothing" and, "I don't want to be a big loser out of the whole affair" rationale. I was desperately trying to keep together my quest for a summer love, but it was wobbling dangerously like a house of cards.

The next week he did call, and I agreed to see him, though without making any promises about the end result of our new evening date. I really wasn't sure what I wanted or how to act. The angel and devil were back in a heated debate on my shoulders, the little angel saying that I shouldn't be seeing him ever, ever again (!), and the naughty devil telling me that I was a 21st-Century woman and should live in the moment (that was one element to the law of attraction after all). The devil also reminded me that I had nothing really to lose. How could Mario truly not be interested in me, after all the chasing he'd done? I still had that little glimmer of hope, and so that rascally devil was gaining terrain.

On the designated evening, Mario came over to my place with a nice bottle of strong, succulent Spanish wine. That helped relax the odd, almost foreboding atmosphere. We talked and laughed, and suddenly the bottle was empty and we headed out for dinner.

Since he was keen to try new places, I took him to a nice bistro in my neighborhood called the *Leopard*. It seemed appropriate for the occasion: a little wild, a little African, and a little Parisian. Another bottle was downed over a somewhat romantic dinner. It might have been the effect of the wine, or maybe it as the little star-shaped lights in the restaurant's ceiling twinkling down at us, but he looked dazzling and I guess so did I. The meal came to an end; savoring the last drops of our wine, we exited the *Leopard* and for a split second there we were—just the two of us—under the real stars of Paris. The *métro* was to the left and my place to the right. Off we went, arm-in-arm . . . to the right.

It hadn't dawned on me at the moment, but it was virtually the same day in October as the first time he'd seduced me two years before. Hadn't I learned my lesson in these two long years?

It was a very passionate night, and the next day I didn't really regret anything. I figured he was finally coming to his senses, and that he would ditch the deadweight. Then we'd be able to see each other! Even though he still hadn't landed the job he wanted (which might have whisked him off to a job in a faraway land), there were still good chances that he would secure a Paris-based job, allowing us to have a happily-ever-after *amour*.

However, the month of November went by at a snail's pace with no word from Mario: no calls, no text messages, no emails, *rien*. I was gradually and painfully snapping out of my dream and coming to the realization that he'd obviously really meant that he just wanted to sleep with me one more time. But why did it have to be only just *one* more time?

I brooded more and more with every passing message-less day. Terrible thoughts and theories nourished a growing regret about letting him get the better of me . . . *again*.

There was no way I was going to contact him; nonetheless, he was consuming my thoughts. Soon, I was having trouble sleeping, tossing and turning, trying to figure out why he'd come back into my life. Was it just to trample all over me a second time? If so, I'd given him an open invitation! I just couldn't understand it. I'd been thinking so positively back in the spring (when I'd first met Jacques and had run into Mario again) that I'd convinced myself that I'd *secret-ed* them into my life and that at least one of these encounters was "meant to be." If this was what *meant to be* was actually supposed to *be,* then I needed to place another order with the Universe, because something had gone terribly wrong! I thought I'd changed my line of thinking! The past three years, I'd transitioned from wanting a "summer fling," to searching for more substance in a "summer romance," and finally to truly craving a "summer love" that would hopefully outlast the summer. However, it seemed that this time around, I'd gotten worse candidates than at the start of my fling quest—I'd ended up attracting not only one . . . but TWO hopeless cases! Furthermore, I'd started to seriously blame myself. How could I have fallen for Mario . . . *twice?* How could I have convinced myself that both Jacques and Mario were "free" and actually wanted to be with me? I was more than disillusioned; I was downright depressed.

It was now into December and the holiday season was approaching. The streets of Paris were dazzling with millions of Christmas lights, and even the grumpiest Parisians were sporting smiles and rosy cheeks. It was practically impossible to not get caught up in the holiday joy; however, I wasn't feeling very merry at all . . . and the negativity building up inside me was about to explode.

Every year the Canadian Club organizes a hike followed by a Christmas party. Those who can survive a daylong trek in a nearby icy forest are treated to hot wine and chili beside the toasty fireplace at the apartment of the club's president. Not surprisingly, I never ventured out on this special hike, but a few lucky non-hikers, such as myself, were always invited to the party anyway.

That Sunday, the thermostat plummeted and a constant drizzle coated the fields and forests of the greater Parisian region of Île-de-France with a slippery frost. I figured there probably wouldn't be too many brave souls attending the hike, and consequently, the after-party. I hemmed and hawed, eventually deciding to trudge down south to the party in the safe, family-friendly 14th arrondissement.

Arriving at the designated time, I rang the doorbell. Nothing. I tried it again, yet no one came to open it. I rang once more, but it remained unanswered. Strange. I put my ear up to the door, to hear that the apartment as eerily quiet— the festivities couldn't have already begun. *Hmmm*, maybe they'd gotten lost in the woods? Stuck in a cold, muddy bog? As I was contemplating how the hikers might have met their sad demise, the building's front door swung open and I was greeted by a freshly-cut, fluffy pine tree, trailed by a small group of shivering hikers, their faces revealed one-by-one by the dim glow of the hallway light.

Lo and behold, a certain jolly Mario was among them. My quickened heartbeat muffled by the welcome "Hellos" and cool-cheeked kisses. I had come to the party because it was a tradition not to be missed, and I really hadn't expected Mario to be attending. *How was I supposed to act?* Avoidance— until I had some hot wine to calm me down—seemed the only logical path. I even offered to be in charge of making it; that would keep me distracted.

Mario did manage to say a proper "Hello" and tell me I looked nice and Christmas-y in my bright red sweater. I couldn't say much to him in reply, I might have forced a meek "thanks" accompanied by a small quivering smile. I was both sad and happy to see him. I was also anguished, not having heard from him in six weeks. As other party-goers gradually trickled in, it became easier to stay out of his way and stay in conversation with someone else, or remain hidden behind the pot of hot wine. By then, I knew that he really had no intentions for us, but as most victims of heartbreak can attest, it's hard to fully accept these sorts of facts and disregard any glimmers of hope that seem to arise. Should I try to flirt with him? I hadn't attended the party with aspirations of seeing him, and I couldn't let his presence ruin my evening. Another glass of hot wine would lighten my spirits. However, I did keep my eye on him, and couldn't help noticing that he was oddly going in and out of the room, making phone calls. Was he expecting someone? Perhaps he'd invited his cousin?

Jovial newcomers kept trickling in and soon the room was full of warmth and cheer. After an hour or so, *I* even started to relax and catch up with old friends from the club. Already knowing most of the guests, it was quite easy to spot anyone new. The club's dapper president always managed to entice some recent attractive shop customers to attend, but there was something out of place with this one pixie-haired blonde who'd just arrived. First of all, she looked French, and the president usually acquired English-speaking admirers. Secondly, she was nowhere near the president, who was by the fireplace charming his new lady friends. Lastly, this other girl seemed to be lingering specifically around Mario.

Who was she? Could she be . . . *his girlfriend?* No, impossible! Mario wouldn't dare bring this possibly-ex-or-not girlfriend to an event that I would be at. Ferocious suspicions were spreading like wildfire across my mind. She was quite pretty, about his age and she was indeed standing right next to him; even if they weren't being lovey-dovey or anything, there was no question that they knew each other. Was I just being unnecessarily jealous?

I struggled to focus on the endless story coming from an extremely talkative woman who'd nailed me down, but now I completely zoned her out. Nodding occasionally, my eyes darted back and forth from her animated face to Mario and the girl. The more I analyzed their behavior, the more I was dead certain that she had to be his girlfriend.

Deep into Ms. Gabby's story, Mario started towards the bathroom. *Should I follow him and confront him there?* I was despairingly trapped in her monologue and couldn't budge. A few minutes later, he reemerged, bee-lining through the crowd back to that girl. It was now or maybe never—I had to know. Cutting Chatty Cathy off in mid-sentence, I accosted Mario.

"Hey Mario, is that your *girlfriend?*" I demanded in a possessed, demonic way.

"Yeah, it is," he said with a resigned look.

"Didn't you think *I might be here?*" I tossed back with more venom that a 15-foot cobra.

In reply, he gave me an even more pathetic and complacent look, shrugged his shoulders and walked away. The talkative witness to this event was finally silenced, her mouth gaping open not with words, but surprise.

Oh my God, was this really happening? How could he have brought her? The reality was that he had never made any effort to break up with her and probably never would. It was like a slap in the face. I felt like a big, huge fool. My churning stomach coupled with the happy laughter of the other guests formed a vicious internal vortex, ready to swallow my remaining sanity whole.

"I have to go," I muttered to the chatterbox, who was still standing there in front of me, wordless. I tried to say as few good-byes as necessary so I could escape before I fainted or caused a dreadfully nasty scene.

I gave my apologies for leaving so early to the club's president on my way out, in exchange for a take-away bowl of chili. I'd so been looking forward to this party, only for it to be ruined by that thoughtless jerk. I was a wreck and was in no condition to stay, but in no condition to go home either. Luckily, Special Kay lived nearby, so I showed up on her doorstep frozen like an emotional popsicle.

"He did *what?*" I told her the whole story, between sobs and attempted bites of my cold chili.

After I'd calmed down a bit, we jointly devised the fiercest text message for Mario (I think the words "asshole" and "dirty pig" were in there, and maybe "rot in hell"), though it would take more than words to stitch up these wounds.

I barely slept that night, the dreary morning eventually dawned and I had to work early. However, I got up even earlier than I had to in order to send Mario an especially evil email, telling him what a pathetic reject he was and demanding a special book (ironically, one written by Jake) that I'd lent him back ASAP—by post; I didn't want to see his disgusting face ever, ever again. When I got home in the evening there was a very brief email simply stating that he'd sent the book back and nothing more. *He had nothing to say for himself?* So I sent him another wrathful message, accusing him of the worst, most cowardly behavior ever demonstrated. Another sleepless night.

When I got home from work the next day I found a lonely, padded envelope sitting in my mailbox; my book accompanied by a long, handwritten letter. An apology of sorts from Mario, claiming he hadn't realized that I really liked him (which was probably true), and admitting to being cowardly with his girlfriend (which was definitely true). He hadn't meant to hurt me, and so on. Over and over, I read the letter—its hastily-written blue words turning into smudges from my cascade of "I had wanted so badly a *je t'aime*" tears.

"Come on, Lily. 'Tis the season to be jolly! Come to *The Reindeer*'s X-mas party tonight!" begged Naughty on my answering machine.

I really wasn't up for *another* Christmas party, especially after the other disastrous one. But I couldn't wallow away at home forever—I needed to get out and I needed to forget. Besides, I hadn't been to *The Reindeer* in ages, and, if nothing else, Julio's smile would give my sad heart a bit of a boost. I put on a shiny scarlet dress, whipped my festive white feather boa around my neck and headed down south on my sleigh/*métro* train.

"Hey there, Sexy Mrs. Claus," greeted Julio. Any iciness that might have enrobed my heart instantly melted. I held onto the bar to maintain my balance as I received a delicate Christmas kiss on each cheek. Maybe Santa could give me a special gift this year? *Caliente* little Julio wrapped in nothing but a big red bow, for example? I certainly deserved it! I was in heaven at the thought. All too soon I was swiftly pulled out of this succulent moment by the bubbly arrival of Ms. Naughty-or-Nice.

"Stop drooling and come sit down," she reprimanded, yanking me over to the table and handing me a Christmas Cosmo.

"Isn't Julio the greatest?" I sighed.

"No he isn't! He's caused you no good at all! Is *he* the only reason you decided to come tonight?" she demanded.

"*Ummm* . . . Of course not . . . we always come to *The Reindeer*'s Christmas party . . ." I sputtered out, trying to recover any dignity I might have actually had left. It wasn't a complete lie; we usually *did* come to the Canadian bar's Christmas party . . . "Still, wasn't Julio totally nice to me just now? He practically gave us our drinks for free."

"You might have a point, but don't forget he never came through before."

Before. It was so easy to forget the start of my quest for a summer fling. And look where it had gotten me. If only Julio had indeed been my real first summer fling . . . I wouldn't have ended up in all this trouble. In all truthfulness, my heart still skipped a beat for Julio—a slightly sorrow-filled beat these days. Another Cosmo would help cure my blues . . . and also give me a chance to chat Julio up a little more. Maybe he didn't have a girlfriend anymore?

As I was about to jump up, three wise men arrived bearing gifts of gold, frankincense and myrrh—or rather, Lieutenant Steve and two of his work colleagues bearing candy canes, mistletoe and Jingle Bell Rock shots. We were soon engrossed in friendly chatter about holiday plans and the latest gossip. I stole a glimpse at Julio whenever I had the chance, dreams of sugarplum Mexicans dancing in my head. Round after round, we enjoyed more than our fair share of holiday cheer. Seeing our glasses empty and no one hanging around the bar, I decided to seize my chance and sauntered tipsily over to bar with the determined aim of re-conquering the Mexican.

"So, what are you doing for the holidays, Lily?" he sweetly asked. "Heading home?"

"No, not this Christmas; I'm off to Milan instead." I almost offered to stow him away in my suitcase. "What about you?"

"Not going anywhere special. But hey, I don't think I told you my big news!" He exclaimed.

Ohhh . . . had he found the piece of paper with my number scrolled on it? Was he on the market and ready to ask me out?

"Big news . . . no, I don't think you told me . . ."

"*I got **married!**"

I don't remember much else about the night other than feigning a congratulatory smile in an attempt to mask my disbelief, downing several more strong shots and somehow ending up fully clothed in my bed at some odd hour of the morning—alone—thus marking the official end to my search for a summer fling, romance or *amour*.

What had happened to my optimistic quest? What began as a little summer adventure turned into three years of turbulent misadventure! Way back at the start, I persevered in spite of: sadly unavailable Julio, departing shepherd-boy Julien, unexpected *papa* Valentino, and Australia-bound Foxy. I'd fended off: over-affectionate Bobbie, inappropriately matched Dean, and blitzing-text-message-warrior Laurent . . . and ahead I ventured. I'd managed to make light of: the ambivalent François, lip-sucking Adil, Mr. Herd of Elephants, and Trick-or-Treat Chris . . . while retaining a glimmer of hope. I'd successfully avoided: mistress-seeking Jean-Claude, the insistent advances of Dave, and falling into Bad Blair's trap yet again . . . and still moved on with my quest. I'd put to the test: the possible and/or definite adulterous actions of *eviling* Jake, the mysterious double-life wiles of Jacques, and the green-eyed seductions of Mario, whose combined deceptions were the last straw. I was through—completely through with them all. However, what had chartered this tumultuous course? It wasn't fair to blame it all on the extremes of Paris's *"Je T'Aime / Me Neither"* vibes.

Since the blow up with Mario, we'd actually exchanged a few emails, which progressively became more and more civil. In one of his messages, he said he would try to be better in the future and that "old dogs could still learn new tricks." I guess I was an old dog, too, one who obviously had many, many lessons to learn. While that may be true, do the lessons have to be taught in such a traumatic way? I suppose that if a message isn't sinking in, we need a big wake up call.

All this time, I hadn't realized that by searching for a summer "fling" that I was attracting just that: mega flings, each one involving very different candidates who were each—in theory—"perfect" fling material. How exciting was a jet fighter pilot? Wasn't a debonair married man ideal for a no-strings-attached affair? Could intense passion in an *aventure* compensate for a short length of time? No, no and no. I didn't want to be swept away with just *anybody*. I couldn't bear becoming a mistress. I didn't really want just a one-weekend *aventure*. I definitely wanted some adventure in life (or even a lot!); however, it was time for me to take responsibility for my fate. I could pray to all the gods I wanted, but the answers really needed to come from inside. I didn't need a "pick-me-up fling" to feel good: I first and foremost needed to love and appreciate myself. Hopefully with some personally *je t'aime*-ing, I might be ready to get back into the adventure of life . . . following a course set out only by me. This was how I could finally find a real *je t'aime*.

However, the first destination on this new path was the refuge of my surrogate Italian family's home for the holidays. It would be the best rehab clinic for my battered heart—far away from the *City of Amour* and certain unsavory male residents. I caught up on my sleep, ate too much pasta, and was happily distracted by my friends.

December 31st was rapidly upon us and we were organizing a big New Year's Eve party. There would be no chance of me getting into any romantic trouble here with my best friend in Milan, Marco. Celebrating with him and his group of mostly gay friends would help me forget the *mauvais* Mario . . . and all the rest of them. Bubbly champagne and *Prosecco* would certainly keep my spirits bright.

The clock was nearing midnight. I looked down into my glass, full of effervescent possibility. I had three years of romantic failures to make up for—a daunting task. Nevertheless, those optimistic little bubbles piped up:

"You can do it, Lily! It's resolution time!" They were right, after all. I had to make some good New Year's resolutions . . . and stick to them this time!

Dieci, nove, otto! With each number of the countdown came a new, powerful resolution in my mind. I was ready for this New Year to commence, and very curious to discover what it had in store for me . . .

. . .

JACQUES [01/01/08 12:04 AM]
Bonne Année ma petite Tigresse!

. . .

DAVE [01/01/08 12:05 AM]
Dear Lily, Happy New Year! You are one of the few people who inspires complete confidence. You will succeed.

Or rather, not *what* it had in store . . . but *who!*

EPILOGUE

[01/21/2008 10:55:08 PM]
DEAN L. says: hey there Lily, you around?

[10:56:34 PM] LILY H. says: Dean! How are YOU?? What's new?

[11:02:03 PM] DEAN L. says: Nothing much, how about you? Meet prince charming yet???

[11:03:27 PM] LILY H. says: hmmmm. . . . not exactly. what about you??? any princesses in your surroundings?

[11:05:17 PM] DEAN L. says: *touché.*

[11:05:31 PM] DEAN L. says: Well, I'm currently very single.

[11:05:52 PM] DEAN L. says: my last relationship ended just before Christmas.

[11:06:45 PM] LILY H. says: Ahhh that's too bad. You'll find someone else soon!

[11:07:51 PM] DEAN L. says: Well maybe, but I do miss the comfort of being in a relationship

[11:10:01 PM] DEAN L. says: how long ago was your last "good" relationship

[11:11:01 PM] LILY H. says: Ha! I can't remember! Not recently anyway!

[11:12:55 PM] DEAN L. says: It's a jungle out there! You know, I'm still a little amazed how we have managed to stay connected . . . maybe it's fate! :)

[11:15:46 PM] DEAN L. says: still there?

[11:15:54 PM] LILY H. says: Yes sorry, I was just working on my book.

[11:19:48 PM] DEAN L. says: your book?

[11:22:09 PM] LILY H. says: ahh yes, it's one of my new year's resolutions. Write my book, do some art and find a new job!

[11:22:15 PM] DEAN L. says: What's it about??

[11:22:20 PM] LILY H. says: I don't know if I can tell you - top secret.

[11:23:43 PM] DEAN L. says: Hmmm . . . that sounds interesting.

[11:24:05 PM] DEAN L. says: maybe a tell-all about former lovers? :)

[11:24:16 PM] LILY H. says: *mayyyybeeeee.*

[11:24:18 PM] LILY H. says: ;)

[11:25:00 PM] DEAN L. says: well, those sound like great resolutions.

[11:25:12 PM] LILY H. says: I'm happy about them - what about you, any resolutions?

[11:25:19 PM] DEAN L. says: do you see yourself living in Paris for the long term?

[11:25:24 PM] DEAN L. says: (loaded question!)
[11:25:49 PM] LILY H. says: hmmmm . . . it's hard to say I don't know where I'll be in the future.

[11:26:25 PM] DEAN L. says: that's not a real answer.

[11:27:16] LILY H. says: ha!

[11:27:26 PM] DEAN L. says: fair enough.

[11:27:30 PM] LILY H. says: well, it depends on where the future takes me!

[11:27:45 PM] LILY H. says: I need to write this book and then we'll see.

[11:45:16 PM] DEAN L. says: are you still up for me visiting sometime? Still thinking about sometime in the late spring or maybe the summer . . .

[11:47:17 PM] LILY H. says: Tempting . . . Summer. Yes, summer would be perfect.

ACKNOWLEDGMENTS

A tremendous thank you must first go to Natasha "Naughty" Frid and Katrin Holt Dubreuil, partners in *je t'aiming*, whose patience, encouragement and, specifically here, editorial assistance have been invaluable throughout this endeavor. Their hard efforts were perfected by the excellent editorial skills of my official editor Samantha Mehra of Ink Think!. All my girls have been absolutely amazing along the way; particular appreciation for their feedback and support must be given to Pascale V. Marquis, Paula McLean, Heather "Cindy" Cowan Desportes, Karin Lynn Bates, Gabie Demers, Tash Ell, Hannah Roberts Celik, Sophie Nellis, Evelyne Rose, Kimberley Pegg, Sara McCarty, Emilie Dingfeld, Riyako Suketomo and Clémence Malaret.

At different stages, I was fortunate and very grateful to have the professional advice of Heather Stimmler Hall, Stephen Clarke, Keith Spicer, Ann Mah and Carolin Young. The book has seen the light of 2013 thanks to Paul Bennett and Lani Bevacqua, who allowed me to take some time off work to wrap up this first opus. The book wouldn't look so beautiful without the artistic talent of Aurélie Dhuit, my cover and interior image designer and Nicolas Beucher, my layout designer. Merci to Romain Gil for keeping the adventures going sporadically over the years, and to a few other *hommes* for their continuous encouragement including: "Lieutenant" Steve Saunders, François Capdeville, Steve Lockie and Giancarlo Pizzi. Thank you to my family for not divorcing me for moving to Paris and for helping foster my creativity and my quest for stories since I was a *toute petite fille*. Lastly, none of this would have been possible without Paris— the backdrop and instigator of these *aventures*.

ABOUT THE AUTHOR

April Lily Heise left her native Canada for Paris in 2000. Ever since, she's been trying—quite unsuccessfully—to stay out of romantic trouble. She's managed to remain in her heart city, subsisting on a variety of jobs, mainly in teaching and tourism. Writing or translating on the side, she has contributed to various travel publications including *Frommer's Paris* and *France* guides and the *Conde Nast Daily Traveler* blog. She has translated large sections of two books by French intellectual Jacques Attali, and wrote two business English language guides. The latter having nothing to do with her current book . . . other than naughtily inspiring one of its chapters. For current musings see: jetaimemeneither.com.

11417835R00172

Made in the USA
San Bernardino, CA
16 May 2014